sixth edition
MASS MEDIA AND SOCIETY

STUDY GUIDE/WORKBOOK

JOURNALISM/COMMUNICATIONS ARTS I

TIM POSADA | J. MICHAEL REED

Kendall Hunt
publishing company

Cover image © Shutterstock, Inc.

Kendall Hunt
publishing company

www.kendallhunt.com
Send all inquiries to:
4050 Westmark Drive
Dubuque, IA 52004-1840

Copyright © 2007, 2008, 2011, 2014, 2016, 2018 by J. Michael Reed and Tim Posada

ISBN 978-1-5249-6276-0

Kendall Hunt Publishing Company has the exclusive rights to reproduce this work, to prepare derivative works from this work, to publicly distribute this work, to publicly perform this work and to publicly display this work.

All rights reserved. No part of this publication may be reproduced, stored in a retrieval system, or transmitted, in any form or by any means, electronic, mechanical, photocopying, recording, or otherwise, without the prior written permission of the copyright owner.

Published in the United States of America

Contents

Introduction		v
Chapter 1	Setting the Academic Agenda	1
Chapter 2	Media Effects/Theory	5
Chapter 3	Yes! The Very Basics	11
Chapter 4	Prior Restraint	17
Chapter 5	Freedom of Expression and Press Responsibility	23
Chapter 6	Privacy Law	27
Chapter 7	Media Ethics	29
Chapter 8	Talk Is Cheap—Free Speech Is Not	33
Chapter 9	Absence of Malice	39
Chapter 10	Newspapers	41
Chapter 11	Media Ownership	45
Chapter 12	Radio/Radio and Politics	53
Chapter 13	Television Programming	57
Chapter 14	Television and Politics	61
Chapter 15	Obscenity and Pornography	65
Chapter 16	Magazines	71
Chapter 17	The Muckrakers	75
Chapter 18	Persuasive Media: Advertising	79
Chapter 19	Persuasive Media: Propaganda	85
Chapter 20	Film	87

Chapter 21	Public Relations	**93**
Chapter 22	Impact of New Media	**97**

List of Resources   **103**

Appendices   **105**

    Journalism Program Goal Statement   **106**

    Course Research Paper   **108**

    Term Project Course Requirements   **110**

    Student Special Project: Native Americans in the Media   **113**

Mass Media and Society Study Guide and Workbook Introduction

This book is meant to serve as a supplement to a mass media text. It emphasizes information that is deemed essential for transfer students to any four-year college or university as a communications/journalism major. However, much of the information has been deemed essential no matter what major a student might select. The content of this study guide is based on more than 30 years of college-level research, teaching experience, and feedback from students.

It is organized in a way that gives students the essentials for media debate and critique. The emphasis is on keeping the information relatively simple with an eye toward certain student learning outcomes. Sections on critical thinking skills and strategies along with an appendix with department goals and course term project assignments are included.

The book's uses student-transfer data and feedback to make sure that students leave the course actually "knowing" certain basic concepts, theories, history, court cases, and ethical issues and standards that will put them in the forefront of their four-year college or university classes.

Constant feedback from former students who have transferred to four-year institutions has been greatly facilitated by the "new media" i.e., Facebook, Twitter, Instagram. This fifth edition features the addition of outside resources like a mass media blog and several links to give students greater and faster access to important elements related to their general education.

Please enjoy!

J. Michael Reed

Setting the Academic Agenda

Chapter 1

This course should be one of the most interesting and fun courses you will take the first two years of college. Every day you live the content of this course. How many hours of television have you watched this week? How many hours have you watched to this point in your life? What impact do you feel television has had on your life? What impact do computers and the Internet have on your life? How have smart phones impacted your life and the lives of your friends? How much time do you spend reading, listening to music? Do you create or download your own music? What impact do the lyrics to songs have on your life? Have you seen a movie in the last couple of weeks? Do you listen to the radio in your car? How do all of these media influence the values and beliefs of Americans and, for that matter, world culture?

Really, you may know as much about the content of this course as your instructor. The instructor will introduce you to the language of media and encourage you to think about the impact of media in a more academic way. You will become students of the media and not just consumers.

Terms

Communication Process:

Messages: source-message-receiver
encoders-channel-decoders
Receivers: Large groups, sometimes world-wide, anonymous, heterogeneous groups.

Blocks to the Communication Process:

Channel Noise: The channel has been interrupted. This may include but not limited to static on radio, cable going out, typo or other errors in books, newspapers. Find other examples.

Semantic Noise: language differences.

Feedback: In our economic system, most of the media is profit driven. Advertisers buy a stake in the messages sent out with the idea they will reap the economic benefits. Let's think about some areas of media feedback that will help us in our discussion of the impact of media on society. Search your media outlets for Nielsen ratings each week. What books are on the NYTimes best seller list? Take note of the Billboard top hits, box office rating for movies, sales of cars, clothes, beer as a result of an advertising campaign. Check for hits on a blog or website. More . . .

More... List Examples

All semester we will be using the terms demographics and psychographics in our discussion of the impact of media in our society.

Demographics: Readily measurable characteristics of audiences such as age, sex, race, income, and level of education.

Psychographics: Internal characteristics of audiences such as values, needs, beliefs, interests, and attitudes.

We can do a demographic survey of our class. Let's think about what we value. What about what we need? What do we believe and what influences our beliefs? What are our attitudes about certain issues? How do we establish attitudes? What influences the way we look at each other and the world? What is the impact of words and images in the media on our life?

Media Segmentation: The proliferation of newspapers, magazines, TV and cable stations, Internet, DVDs, CDs, and more give consumers many more choices and makes it hard for any one media to dominate the market.

Media Convergence: Large corporations that are content providers buy up more of the means to distribute and control that content. Large media mergers can give large corporations the ability to control content in a way never seen before.

PQ and CQ: Passion Quotient/Curiosity quotient.

Thomas L. Friedman, <u>The World Is Flat 2.0,</u> a **MUST** read for college students.

What will you do to make sure you are able to compete for a job with students around the globe? Many job seekers in other countries may be willing to work twice as hard for less pay.

High Tech/High Touch: The more technologically advanced we become, the more we yearn for the human touch. Example: Movie theaters vs. Home DVD or Netflix.

Models for Your Consideration

$—Power (education, knowledge)
Words—Images-Thought-Action
Power of the media

Study Guide Questions

How many hours a week do you read? (print media, magazines, newspapers, textbooks, etc.)
Do you access news on your smart phone or other devices?
How many hours a week do you spend online?

>Reading news: (Online, via cell phone, TV)
>(Recommended online news source: AP (app)
>Associated Press for your smartphones or tablets.

Gives news alerts to your home page.
Facebook:
Instagram
Email:
YouTube:
Playing games:
Doing research for classes:
Other:

Have you or do you gamble online? Should online gambling be legal?

How much television do you watch on an average day?

What are your favorite programs and why?

How much time do you spend listening to a radio? Favorite programs or stations?

How much time do you spend on your smart phone each day?

How much time, on average, do you spend listening to MP3 player?

Do you watch TV programs on your MP3 player? If so which programs?

How many movies do you watch in a month? Favorite genre of movie?

List three things you value most:

List any strong beliefs:

List your main needs in life:

What are your main interests?

Do you think advertisers, movie producers, television producers, and other media gatekeepers are interested in the above items you listed? Why?

Student Notes

Chapter 2

Media Effects/Theory

The course title is Mass Media and Society, so it is important to include a general survey of a few of the theories about the impact of media on society. These theories include but are not limited to those listed here. Each will be briefly reviewed and discussed in class lecture. Please review your course text to prepare for discussion on these and other related theories.

Media theory deals with the process of media communication. Discussions will include why and how people receive and interpret these messages. How do people use these messages and what are the psychological, social, and cultural effects of these mass produced messages?

Media Functions: Inform, persuade, entertain, and transmit culture. Other terms used to describe functions that will be used in class: surveillance, interpretation, correlation, linkage, and more.

Process: Source (encoder)—message (channel)—receivers (decoder)

Terms

1. **Cognitive Needs:** Human needs to gain knowledge and understanding.
2. **Affective Needs:** Human needs for aesthetic, pleasurable, and emotional experiences.

Other needs discussed under the psychographic function of media could include our need to strengthen and evaluate values related to family, friends, our country, the world.

Through the entertainment function, needs related to escape, tension, release, and diversion may be addressed. Other functions will be discussed in later sections related to the theories and philosophies of Abraham Maslow and others.

Harold Lasswell, communication theorist, helped frame this issue:

"Who says what, to whom, through what channel, with what effect."

Direct Effects Theory (Bullet Theory): Propaganda and advertising campaigns can be very effective. Powerful messages in movie and television programming have strong impacts on society.

Individual Differences/Limited Effects Theory: Individual's values, needs, beliefs, and attitudes play a major role.

Social Learning Theory/Observed Learning and Modeling Theory: We learn from observing and modeling in the media and from direct experience as well.

Cultivation Theory: Television is partially responsible for shaping or "cultivating" a viewer's understanding of social reality.

Agenda Setting Theory: News influences our perception of the world.

> *FOX News*: Jan 18, 2006, 3:20 p.m.
> Setting the agenda for a U.S. attack on Iran that included maps of targets, weapons, and ordinance to be used. Brit Hume, "news" anchor or commentator? Magazines that set the agenda for debate on fashion, design, diet, and more.

Theories for further research and your consideration: Play theory, expectancy theories.

Marshall McLuhan

The father of media studies, McLuhan is best known for the phrase, "The medium is the message," also the title of the first chapter in his quintessential work *Understanding Media: The Extensions of Man*, where he theorizes the technology becomes "extensions" of our body that expand our reach. If you recall, medium is the singular of media. And the message is considered the material in a communication model. To consider the meaning of this phrase, let's once again construct a message.

For example, if a student were to text a professor, that professor might not respond since such a form of communication could be deemed too informal for a student/professor relationship. But if that student emailed the professor through a college-specific email address, the professor might respond as soon as possible. Considering folks use their phones for everything, there is no practical reason to respond quickly to one and ignore the other. On a smartphone, both are received with the same device. But if "the medium is the message," then a clear symbolic difference exists between a text message and an email. There might be a practical reason for my email preference, like documenting all exchanges with students. (Who knows when you might need to look them up?) But the real reason is that text messaging as a "medium" changes the way people construct a "message."

The tools might appear similar, but email is a more formal communication process. In an email, a message from a might say, "Dear Professor Posada, I apologize for missing class today. I was out sick. I was wondering if you could inform me as to what I missed." This is far more formal than a text message that reads, "Hey bro, what did I miss in class today?!" (That last example is not fake; it really happened.)

For McLuhan, the medium often spoke louder than raw content. Every medium has different parameters. Twitter, part of the broader medium of the internet, limits communication to 280 characters (once only 140). Snapchat shows images that go away after 10 seconds. Films average 80 to 180 minutes. Films can be any length they want, but the *norm* (it would be odd to spend $13.50 on a 30-minute film) establishes how that message is constructed.

"The medium is the message" should become second nature to you. Look it up in more detail and better understand what it means for media that continue to change.

Topics for Discussion

Effects of advertising on children: What do you think?
Do ads for children's programs blur the line between program content and advertising?

Effects of violence in the media: Violence/conflict/human drama—Violence embodies conflict and conflict is the heart and soul of drama. There are many different levels of conflict. When does it rise to the level of violence? What do you think?

What is the impact of video game violence? Go to http://www.cbsnews.com/60-minutes/ and search for segments they have produced related to video game violence.

Desensitization: Repeated exposure to media violence causes a reduction in emotional response. How does this affect our feeling regarding news reports on war fronts?
Daily there are headlines in the media outlets about bombings and loss of life, not to mention the many maimed or injured in Iraq, Afghanistan, Syria, Libya, Egypt, and so on.
Fox News ALERT! ALERT! ALERT! Repeated for so many stories just to keep us on "Alert" and watching the network. The network had to come up with another word when something really terrible happens: Fox News URGENT. (Killings at the Virginia Naval Yard 2013)

Chapter 2 Media Effects/Theory

Effects of sexually explicit materials on society: What do you think? Online pornography may be affecting marital relationships.

Effects of underrepresentation or misrepresentation of minorities in the media: What do you think?

Justice by television: Do you think people judge people by what is reported in the news rather than in the courts? Most of the morning talk shows host people involved in legal issues and then the networks have their own "legal experts", tell you how the case will evolve and be resolved. How does this information affect 6th Amendment rights?

Politics by television: Do you feel political ads should be more regulated?
Can you really believe what you are exposed to in most political ads or should you do some more research to get the facts?

The impact of Internet gambling on society: What do you think? Should gambling online be legal in the United States?

The impact of online pornography on society: What do you think the impact is and where would you draw the line? Go to 60 Mins.com and do a search for programs they have done on the impact of sexually explicit material on society.

Chapter 2   Media Effects/Theory | 9

The impact of smart phone technology on society:
Your class can write the results of this impact.

Polarization of America: What is the media's role?
Do the media love the "red" states and the "blue" states? Do the media like conflict? Do they like to frame issues as black and white? Does that make debate on important issues easier for most Americans to understand?
Young v Old
Minority v White
Secular v Religious
Liberal v Conservative
Urban v Rural

As you view "news" on the television networks, see how many times the news anchor asks during an interview, for a RESPONSE or a REACTION. Is there a difference?

Define acculturation:

Student Notes

Chapter 3

Yes! The Very Basics

We, the people of the United States, in order to form a more perfect union, establish justice, insure domestic tranquility, provide for the common defense, promote the general welfare, and secure the blessings of liberty to ourselves and our posterity, do ordain and establish this Constitution of the United States of America.

The Constitution established three estates of power.

Legislative

Legislates. Makes the laws under which WE THE PEOPLE live.

Congress:

- House of Representatives
- Senate

Executive

Executes the laws. President of the United States and his or her staff.

The oath to be taken by the president upon first entering office is specified in Article II, Section 1 of the U.S. Constitution:

*"I do solemnly swear (or affirm) that I will faithfully execute the office of President of the United States, and will to the best of my ability, preserve, protect, and defend the **Constitution** of the United States."*

Judicial

Determines if the laws are in keeping with our National Constitution.

Estates of Power: Legislative, executive, judicial, press, lobbyists.

First Amendment to the U.S. Constitution

CONGRESS SHALL MAKE NO LAW *respecting an establishment of religion, or prohibiting the free exercise thereof; or abridging the freedom of speech, or of the press; or the right of the people peaceably to assemble, and to petition the government for a redress of grievances.*

There were four basic freedoms that the former colonists wanted guaranteed before they would sign on to this new federal government. A fifth implicit freedom guaranteed here was "the public's right to know."

Many citizens feel that the First Amendment to the Constitution established a fourth power block: the **media**.

A case can be made that lobbyists now represent another major power block in our government, a potential fifth estate if you will.

The media, empowered by the First Amendment, acts as a check and balance for all the other power blocks.

Resource: *Miracle at Philadelphia* by Catherine Drinker Bowen.
From a meeting at the Pennsylvania State House in 1787 to the ratification of the document, the making of the U.S. Constitution was a true "miracle" of history.
Among the 55 delegates to the constitutional convention were: George Washington, James Madison, Alexander Hamilton, Ben Franklin and Patrick Henry.
Twelve delegates stayed in Philadelphia through that first summer.

Fourth Amendment to the U.S. Constitution

The right of the people to be secure in their persons, houses, papers, and effects, against unreasonable searches and seizures, shall not be violated, and no warrants shall issue, but upon probable cause, supported by Oath or affirmation, and particularly describing the place to be searched, and the persons or things to be seized.

Sixth Amendment to the U.S. Constitution

In all criminal prosecutions, the accused shall enjoy the right to a speedy and public trial, by an IMPARTIAL (emphasis author's) *jury of the state and district wherein the crime shall have been committed, which district shall have been previously ascertained by law, and to be informed of the nature and cause of the accusation; to be confronted with the witnesses against him; to have compulsory process for obtaining witnesses in his favor, and to have the assistance of counsel for his defense.*

Fourteenth Amendment to the U.S. Constitution (Ratified July 9, 1868)

Section 1 of 5. *All persons born or naturalized in the United States and subject to the jurisdiction thereof are citizens of the United States and of the state wherein they reside.*

No State shall make or enforce any law which shall abridge the privileges or immunities of citizens of the United States; nor shall any state deprive any person of life, liberty, or property, without due process of law; nor deny to any person within its jurisdiction the equal protection of the laws.

Four Theories of the Press

How shall information be disseminated in a society?

Authoritarian: Private ownership of the means to disseminate. Government uses techniques such as licensing and taxation to monitor and control the media.
Plato (c. 427–347 B.C.E) said that even an enlightened society must be supervised by the wisest and strongest, i.e., rule by the educated, rich, and powerful. Niccoló Machiavelli's *The Prince* (1513) argues that the ends justify the means.
   1712, The Stamp Act

Sedition: Criticism of the state

Totalitarian: The government owns the presses.

Libertarian: John Stuart Mill, *On Liberty* (1859), "right of mature individuals to think and act as they please so long as they do not hurt someone else." Introduced the idea of *utilitarianism* or the greatest happiness for the greatest number of people.
   John Milton (1644), "Let all with something to say be free to express themselves. Let truth and falsehood grapple; whoever knew truth to be worse in a free and open encounter . . . though all the winds of doctrine were let loose to play upon the earth, so truth be in the field, we do injuriously by licensing and prohibiting, to misdoubt her strength," from a speech "Appeal for the Liberty of Unlicensed Printing." (*Areopagitica*)

President Thomas Jefferson:

> *"The basis of our government being the opinion of the people, the very first object should be to keep that right; and were it left to me to decide whether we should have a government without newspapers, or newspapers without a government, I should not hesitate a moment to prefer the latter."*

Social Responsibility: 1940s Commission on Freedom of the Press, a socially responsible press seeks to protect free expression of individuals in all manners of mass communication and requires the media to represent all points of view on the social spectrum. It promotes media ethics and responsibility.
   The 1942 Hutchins Commission named after University of Chicago Chancellor Robert M. Hutchings, who was the chair of the commission. The commission was funded by Henry Luce (Time/Life) and the *Encyclopedia Britannica*.

Three fundamental positions:

1. Whoever enjoys freedom has certain obligations to society.
2. Society's welfare becomes the most overriding concern. An individual's rights to speak out are balanced by group rights to be free from invasion of privacy or libel; personal rights to free expression are described in terms of public access to the media, or the "public's right to know."
3. Media, as a matter of policy, carry views contrary to their own.

14 | Chapter 3 Yes! The Very Basics

Do an Online Search For:

Jodi Arias trial (spring, summer 2013)
Trial of Michael Jackson's doctor
Trial of George Zimmerman (Florida 2013)
Amada Knox
Rodney King
O.J. Simpson

List cases the news media are covering now, that give information that may influence a defendant's right to an impartial jury.

What can judges do to insure that a defendant's Sixth Amendment rights are protected?

What rights to police officers have when it comes to searches and seizures?

What rights do you have?

The courts are reviewing cases related to officers taking your smart phone after a traffic stop and searching for information that may lead to other charges.

Study Guide Questions

Possible essay question:

What is the conflict between the First and Sixth Amendments to the U.S. Constitution? In your answer include the freedoms quarantined by each amendment and then discuss the inherent conflict. (Think public's right to know vs. fair and speedy trial by an IMPARTIAL jury.)

List at least five of the many functions specific to the legislature branch listed in the U.S. Constitution.

List five functions given specifically to the executive branch by the U.S. Constitution.

List the nine Supreme Court Justices today.

Give two examples pointing out the conflict between the "public's right to know" and the right of a citizen to a fair and speedy trial by an impartial jury.

Do you feel the media is too invasive of public figures' lives? Give an example to support your point of view.

Chapter 3 Yes! The Very Basics

Why do you think Thomas Jefferson thought the citizens of this country would be better off in a system with newspapers?

Do police have the right to conduct warrantless searches of data on a smart phone during a traffic stop?

Prior Restraint

Chapter 4

Even though our First Amendment is viewed as very libertarian in nature, our government has determined that it is not absolute under all circumstances.

Schenck v United States 1919

Schenck was an important case placing limits on the First Amendment right to freedom of expression.

The first five words of the First Amendment to the Constitution: Congress shall make NO (emphasis author's) law . . . restricting freedom of speech . . .

The United States' decision to enter World War I presented some interesting challenges to citizens' First Amendment rights.

We the People passed the **Espionage Act** (1917) two months after America declared war on Germany. The Act was amended in May 1918. The Act said that . . . "whoever, for the purpose of obtaining information respecting the national defense with intent or reason to believe that the information to be obtained is to be used to the injury of the United States or within the exclusive jurisdiction of the United States or any place in which any vessel, aircraft, arms, munitions, or other materials or instruments for use in time of war are being made, prepared, repaired. Whoever, being entrusted with or having lawful possession or control of any document or information, are in violation of trust, or to be listed, stolen, abstracted, or destroyed shall be punished by a fine of not more the $10,000 or by imprisonment for not more than two years or both."

The **Sedition Act** of 1918: Whoever, when the United States is at war, shall willfully make or convey false reports or false statements with intent to interfere with the operation or success of the military or naval forces of the United States or to promote the success of its enemies, or shall willfully make or convey false reports or false statements or say or do anything except by way of bona fide and not disloyal advice to an investor or investors . . .

> "Shall willfully cause or attempt to cause, or incite or attempt to incite, insubordination, disloyalty, mutiny, or refusal of duty, in the military or naval forces of the United States and whoever, when the United States is at war, shall **willfully utter, print, write or publish** any disloyal, profane, scurrilous, or abusive language about the form of government of the United States or the Constitution of the United States, or the military or naval forces of the United States, or the flag of the United States, or the uniform of the Army or Navy of the United States into contempt, scorn, contumely, or disrepute . . . and whoever shall by word or act support or favor the cause of any country with which the United States is at war or by word or act oppose the cause of the United States shall be punished by a fine of not more than $10,000 . . ."

Chapter 4 Prior Restraint

About 900 Americans were imprisoned in the months after the Act was passed by Congress. Eugene V. Debs was sentenced to ten years for a speech in Canton, Ohio, on June 16, 1918 attacking the Espionage Act.

Many citizens were opposed to the United States' involvement in WW I. Among them was Charles Schenck, General Secretary of the Socialist Party. He and his staff produced and distributed 15,000 leaflets urging young men not to register for the newly enacted draft, saying that the draft was a violation of their 13th Amendment rights. His offices were raided by the federal government and he was arrested, charged and convicted with violating the Espionage and Sedition Acts. Schenck's attorney appealed the case to the Supreme Court on the basis that the laws were overly restrictive of citizens' First Amendment rights and thus unconstitutional.

Chief Justice Edward Douglas White asked Justice Oliver Wendell Holmes to write the majority opinion in *Schenck v United States* (emphasis added):

*"We admit that in many places and in **ordinary** times (Schenck) in saying all that was said in the circular would have been within (his) constitutional rights. But the character of every act depends upon the **circumstances** in which it is done. The most stringent protection of free speech would not protect a man in **falsely shouting fire in a theatre**, and causing a panic. It does not even protect a man from injunction (order to stop) against uttering words that may have all the effect of force. The question in every case is whether the words used are used in such circumstances and are of such a nature **as to create a clear and present danger** that they will bring about the substantive evils that Congress has a right to prevent. It is a question of proximity and degree."*

"When a nation is at war many things that might be said in time of peace are such a hindrance to its effort that their utterance will not be endured so long as men fight and that no court could regard them as protected by any constitutional right."

Many authoritarian governments have attempted to restrict the flow of information. England's Henry VIII initiated methods such as licensing printing presses. In 1765, the British imposed the Stamp Act on the colonists. Under the British system, sedition or any criticism of the government was illegal.

Near v Minnesota 1931 (U.S. Supreme Court)

In 1925, the Minnesota state legislature passed a law that allowed government authorities to halt publication of any obscene, lewd, and lascivious ... or malicious, scandalous, and defamatory newspaper, magazine, or other periodical as a public nuisance.

Jay Near and Howard Guilford used their newspaper, the *Saturday Press*, to accuse government officials of ignoring widespread racketeering, bootlegging, and illegal gambling. The newspaper was accused of being sensational and anti-Semitic in its hard-hitting articles. The county attorney filed a criminal complaint against the paper and a judge found Near and Guilford in violation of the state statute and ordered them to stop publication of the *Saturday Press* and enjoined them from starting up any like newspaper.

The Minnesota Supreme Court upheld the lower court conviction and the case went to the U.S. Supreme Court who reversed the conviction holding that the state law was overly restrictive of citizens' First Amendment rights. This case was also significant because the justices held that the First Amendment right is not absolute and that there were still circumstances that might justify a government prior restraint.

Pentagon Papers 1971

The executive branch of the government commissioned the Rand Corporation to conduct a study on how the United States got involved in Vietnam. The result was a document titled "A History of the U.S. Decision Making Process on Vietnam Policy."

Daniel Ellsberg had worked on the document and determined that the information contained therein was something the American public had a right to know. He leaked information from the top-secret study to the editors of the *New York Times*. Other newspapers picked up the story. The government went to the Supreme Court to get a restraining order to stop publication of the report. An injunction was issued and later withdrawn when the Supreme Court reviewed the information and concluded that, yes, rather than being condemned for their reporting, the newspapers should be commended for their courage in reporting the information that was of such importance to the American people.

Progressive Magazine Case 1979

Howard Morland researched and wrote a story on how easy it was to get information on how to build a hydrogen bomb. The government found out about the story and sought to ban its publication. The Justice Department filed suit in a federal court and obtained a temporary restraining order against publication of the article. The case was dropped before it reached the U.S. Supreme Court.

Hazelwood v Kuhlmeier 1987 (U.S. Supreme Court)

The case arose from a suit by journalism students at Hazelwood East High School in Missouri. They went to court after their principal, Robert E. Reynolds, deleted two pages from the May 13, 1983 issue of the *Spectrum*, a student newspaper produced as part of an elective course called Journalism II. Reynolds pulled the pages because of two stories about teen pregnancy and divorce. In his view, the articles did not adequately disguise the identities of girls who had been pregnant or the anonymity of a parent who was getting divorced. Further, he said references in the first story to sexual activity and birth control were inappropriate for younger students to read.

In a 5-3 ruling, the Supreme Court gave school administrators broad latitude to suppress controversial stories. **"A school need not tolerate student speech that is inconsistent with its 'basic educational mission',"** Justice Byron White wrote for the majority. School officials may impose reasonable restrictions on the speech of students, teachers, and other members of the school community.

Tinker v Des Moines Independent Community School Dist. 1969 (U.S. Supreme Court)

John Tinker, 15 years old, his sister Mary Beth Tinker, 13 years old, and Christopher Echardt, 16 years old, decided along with their parents to protest the Vietnam War by wearing black armbands to their Des Moines schools during the Christmas holiday season. Upon learning of their intentions, and fearing that the armbands would provoke disturbances, the principals of the Des Moines school district resolved that all students wearing armbands be asked to remove them or face suspension. When the Tinker siblings and Christopher wore their armbands to school, they were asked to remove them. When they refused, they were suspended until after New Year's Day.

The Supreme Court said:

The wearing of armbands was "closely akin to 'pure speech'" and protected by the First Amendment. School environments imply limitations on free expression, but here the principals lacked justification for imposing any such limits. The principals had failed to show that the forbidden conduct would substantially interfere with appropriate school discipline.

Do an online search for more information on the court case and give your opinion here.

Do Online Research on the Following:

California Assembly Bill 2581 which took effect Jan 1, 2007. Explain the reason for the bill and give your opinion. This bill relates to state law affecting high school student's First Amendment rights.

United States v Reynolds **1953 (U.S. Supreme Court)** How do you feel about the ability of the executive branch to withhold information the public may have the "right to know?"

War Powers Act **1975:** Under what circumstances may the President go to war without the approval of Congress and how long can he keep troops in harm's way without Congressional approval?

Morse et al. v Fredrick **2007 (U.S. Supreme Court)**
"*Bong Hits 4 Jesus*": Go to the course blog for more info on this case. Select one court opinion which was NOT a majority opinion and discuss. Student rights to freedom of expression.

The "I Love Boobies" bracelet case: ***Easton Area School District v Brianna Hawk and Kayla Martinez*, 2013.** Student rights to freedom of expression.

WikiLeaks:

Julian Assange 2010–11
Research this topic and write a one-page summary including your opinion based on the court cases you have studied so far. (Attach the typed opinion to this study guide page with a staple)

Edward Snowden 2013–
Former CIA information technical assistant who leaked classified material about NSA's secret programs to collect phone records and Internet data on American citizens as well as foreign leaders.

Ongoing conflict between Apple Co. and the U.S. Government regarding encryption codes protecting IPhone user's privacy.

Should the government be able to force Apple to create a way to access the phone records of private individuals, with a warrant, when national security is threatened? This is an ongoing issue at the time this edition of the study guide is published.

Study Guide Issues for Discussion

What about the government's reluctance to release information related to?
- The Vietnam War
- The Gulf War
- The Iraq War
- Afghanistan War
- War on Terror

Study Guide Questions

Under what circumstances do you feel the government of the United States has the right or obligation to censor information in which the public may have an interest?

Do you agree with the principles established by the *Hazelwood v Kuhlmeier* case? Explain why yes or no.

Chapter 4 Prior Restraint

Do you see parallels between the rights of the media during the current international conflict and the principles involved in the *Schenck v U.S.* case?

Please attach typed double-spaced responses to the required research topics on this page, as you cannot respond in the original space provided.

Freedom of Expression and Press Responsibility

Chapter 5

Terms

Libel: False published defamation
Slander: False spoken defamation

Four Elements of Libel:
1. **Defamation**–hurt ones' reputation, damage their earning power, hold them up to ridicule, make them seem ridiculous, cause them to be shunned.
2. **Identification**–not necessarily just a name needed.
3. **Publication**–must be in print or broadcast.
4. **Negligence**–plaintiff must show that the media did not do their job right. They did not act reasonably or as one might expect them to act.

Four Best Defenses Against a Libel Suit:
1. **Truth**—This is the number one defense in the United States. Is the information TRUE and can you prove it is true? Should it be required by a judge?
2. **Privilege**—Is the information "a matter of public record"? Is the information taken from sources the "public has the right to know"? The Congressional Record, Board of Trustee minutes, Associated Student Government meeting records, budget of public institutions and more are examples. Court records are also public record unless a judge seals them.
3. **Fair comment and critics**—If a person is "in the public light," a movie star, athlete, elected official etc., they are open to critique by the media.

Note: *Milkovich v Lorain Journal Co.* 1990

The Supreme Court noted in this case that in some circumstances opinions may often imply an assertion of objective fact. William Rehnquist speaking for the majority reversed a lower court ruling that had supported columnist Ted Diadium's assertion, in a sports column, that a high school wrestling coach lied to a judge about a brawl that took place after a match between two teams, was protected under the fair comment and criticism defense against libel.

As a result of the fight, the state (Ohio) athletic board placed the teams on probation which would have precluded participation in the playoffs. Parents went to court to get the ban lifted which they did after testimony from the coach and principal of the school was given to absolve the leadership of responsibility in the conflict. Diadium subsequently wrote the column critical of the testimony and behavior of the coach. **The Supreme Court ruled in the case that assertions of criminal wrongdoing may not be protected opinion.**

4. **Absence of Malice**— Since the 1964 *New York Times Co. v Sullivan* Supreme Court case, public figures and public officials must prove that the media acted with actual malice before they can win damages in a libel suit. In other words, the plaintiffs must prove in court that the media knew ahead of time that the information they published was false and defamatory and printed it anyway. Justice William Brennan, writing for the majority, said that the media may need some "breathing space" in performing the functions the founding fathers sought when they drafted the First Amendment to the Constitution.

    The original case (*Sullivan v New York Times Co.*) revolved around an advertisement placed in the Times by the Committee to Support Dr. Martin Luther King and the Struggle for Freedom in the South.

    The $4,800 full-page ad was critical of the tactics used by the Montgomery, Alabama police in addressing a protest by students held at Alabama State University. The ad accused the police of intimidating the students. There were 650,000 issues published. There were 394 subscribers in Alabama and 35 subscribers in Montgomery County.

    Attorneys for Police Commissioner L.B. Sullivan were able to point out several falsehoods in the ad that were defamatory.

    1. The ad said the students were on the steps of the administration building singing "My County Tis of Thee" when they were singing "The Star Spangled Banner."
    2. The ad said that the police surrounded the campus. They did not. The ad stated that the police padlocked the dinning hall to starve the students into submission.
    3. The ad said Dr. Martin Luther King had been arrested seven times (the *Times'* own recorders supported that he had only been arrested four times) Other details were not exactly correct and the attorneys were able to bring witnesses to the stand that felt that Sullivan was the person being criticized.

The Montgomery Court awarded Sullivan the $500,000 in damages he had sued for. The Alabama Supreme Court upheld the ruling. The U.S. Supreme Court reversed the lower courts' findings in this case.

Go to the course blog for video on this issue.

Do an Online Search For:

Twibel Case: Defamatory information posted on Twitter

Gordon and Holmes vs. Love **case**
In 2010, Courtney Love accused her former attorney Ronda Holms of bribery.
"I was f _____ devastated when Ronda J. Holmes esq. of San Diego was bought off."

In Love's case, the Twitter user, not the social media site is liable for the defamation. As a third-party publisher, social media sites such as Twitter are protected by Section 230 of the Communication Decency Act

Sarah Jones, former Cincinnati Bengals cheerleader *v The Dirty.com*

Study Guide Activities

Do a computer search for court cases dealing with who is a public figure or official for the purposes of a libel lawsuit. What were the results?

Do a search to locate any recent libel cases related to media personalities. What were the results?

Do you feel the *New York Times Co. v Sullivan* case gives the media too much freedom? Why yes/why no?

Do an informal survey (25 people) to see if they feel the media has too much freedom in America or not enough.

List names of publications you feel most often push the boundaries of libelous speech.

Student Notes

Privacy Law

Chapter 6

Fourth Amendment U.S. Constitution

The right of the people to be secure in their persons, houses, papers, and effects, against unreasonable searches and seizures, shall not be violated, and no warrants shall issue, but upon probable cause, supported by oath or affirmation, and particularly describing the place to be searched, and the persons or things to be seized.

Harvard Law Review Essay by Samuel D. Warren and Louis D. Brandeis 1890 (later a Supreme Court Justice)

They put forth the concept that there should be aright of privacy either under the common law or state statutory law regarding an individual's "right to privacy."

This right should protect prominent persons from gossipy reporting of their private affairs.

"The press is overstepping in every direction the obvious bounds of propriety and decency. Gossip is no longer the resource of the idle and of the vicious, but has become a trade, which is pursued with industry as well as effrontery."

Appropriation: Protects individuals from unauthorized commercial use of their names, photographs, and other aspects of their public persona. (face, body, voice, etc.)

Intrusion: Unduly intruding into ones' physical solitude or seclusion or private affairs. Snooping, eavesdropping or intruding into someone's reasonable right to peace and quiet.

Example:

Jackie Onassis: Photographer Ron Gallela took a photo 24 feet from Jackie and 30 feet from her children.

False Light: Do not put people in a false light. Do not take something in one context and put it into another context especially if the new context may be defamatory.

Private Facts: Private information that may be offensive to a reasonable person. Not of legitimate public interest.

Chapter 6   Privacy Law

Do an Online Search For:

1974 Privacy Act

Ron Galella

Jackie Onassis

Vanessa Williams

Sean Penn

Other privacy suits by major public figures

Erin Andrews v Michael Barrett and Marriott 2016

Hulk Hogan v Gawker 2016

Video Voyeurism Act 2004: Case regarding disseminating images of a "person's private parts" when the person has a reasonable expectation of privacy regardless of private or public location. Note the actual provisions of the act and list them here.

Can a person take a picture of you anywhere, any time?

Please refer to your textbook and/or do an online search for the latest laws regarding Copyright. What would constitute "fair use" of copyrighted material?

Who owns a tattoo? Professional athletes now having to ask for copyright waivers from tattoo artists.

Do an online search for the SCOTUS case: **Utah vs Strieff** 2016 (regards police right to stop and search) At the time this case was scheduled for hearing, Justice Antonin Scalia had just died leaving the course with 8 justices. If there is a 4/4 deadlock, the case could be reverted back to the Utah Supreme Court. How did that court rule in this case.

Kentucky V. King SCOTUS
What did the court say regarding warrantless searches?

Media Ethics

Chapter 7

A sense of what is right and what is wrong is essential to a society dedicated to justice and equality for all. **Aristotle**, the esteemed Greek philosopher, initiated the "golden mean" a philosophy espousing the concept of avoiding extremes and seeking more moderate means. The media concept of being fair and balanced comes from this basic principle.

German philosopher **Immanuel Kant** (1724–1804) developed the concept of the "categorical imperative." He sought a more philosophical approach to issues related to ethical behavior and decision making. He thought people need not dictate what is right or wrong in every circumstance. Hard thinking, debate, and discussion can lead to a common good based on input from as many sources as we can gather. This theory exhorts people to identify and apply universal principles, i.e., to find principles that most people would be comfortable living with in most situations. The ethical codes that journalism associations develop could be put in this classification.

British-born **John Stuart Mill**, in the mid-1800s, came up with what became the basis for the libertarian concept related to social and political philosophy. Basic to this concept was the idea that people should be able to think and do pretty much what they want as long as they do not hurt someone else. The concept correlates with our democratic principle of majority rule. The emphasis is on the greatest good for the greatest number of people.

This utilitarian philosophy supports the journalistic concept of "the people's right to know." This concept puts the public interest ahead of government interests. This concept is alive and well today with the Libertarian Party. *The Orange County Register* newspaper has been called the flagship publication of the Libertarian Party. Adherents to this philosophy want a limited role of government in business and social issues. They also are strong adherents of the strict interpretation of the U.S. Constitution. The term "laissez-faire" applies here in that, economically, libertarians want the market place to dictate business climates, not government regulation.

Through online or other resources, define the following terms:

Plagiarism: The practice of taking someone else's work and using it without permission.

Junkets:

Freebies:

Payola:

Plugola:

On/Off the Record:

Shield laws: Laws that protect reporter's sources or confidential information.

Again, **do online research on:**

Janet Cooke:
"Jimmy is 8 years old and a third-generation heroin addict, a precocious little boy with sandy hair, velvety brown eyes and needle marks freckling the baby-smooth skin of his thin brown arms."

Cooke, who was 25 at the time, won the Pulitzer Prize for this article, "Jimmy's World." Her resume listed a BA from Vassar, magna cum laude (she attended one year). The University of Toledo had no record of her earning a master's degree there.

"Jimmy's World" was published in September 1980. The AP (Associated Press) started the investigation into her background after she was named a Pulitzer Prize winner. Lead to *Washington Post* article by Janet Cooke, "Jimmy's World."

Check the course blog for more info

Study Guide Activities

Rent and view the movie *Shattered Glass*. What are the ethical issues involved? What were the results and consequences of these issues?

Do a computer search on Jason Blair, *New York Times* reporter. What were the ethical issues involved? What were the results and consequences of these issues?

Do an online search for 2013 Fox News reporter Jana Winter. She had written a exclusive story regarding the contents of a notebook belonging to the Aurora, Colorado shooting suspect James Holes. Where was the case heard and why?

Do a computer search for journalism "Codes of Ethics."

What protection do Bloggers have when ordered to give up sources?
Search online for blogger Robert "KC" Johnson
He had posted information regarding a Duke University lacrosse team rape case.

Do research to find out the policies of two of your local newspapers with regard to accepting freebies or free trips.

Movies dealing with these issues you may want to rent or view through online sources:
All the President's Men
Spotlight
Absence of Malice

Student Notes

Talk Is Cheap—Free Speech Is Not

Chapter 8

The Supreme Court, while outlining some limits to free speech, ruled on cases that limited government's latitude in limiting citizens' freedom of expression.

Chaplinsky v New Hampshire 1942 (U.S. Supreme Court)

New Hampshire had an ordinance that said you shall not address words that are offensive, derisive, or annoying to anyone lawfully in a public place, nor call him by any offensive or derisive name.

Walter Chaplinsky, a Jehovah's Witness, was arrested for "evangelizing" on the "harlot" Catholic Church and on saluting the flag. Local citizens called the police because Chaplinsky was causing a disturbance. When arrested, he called the marshal a "God damned racketeer" and a "damned Fascist" and the whole government of Rochester Fascists or agents of Fascists. Chaplinsky was arrested for violating the above ordinance.

Justice Murphy, writing for the majority, said: the "right of free speech is not absolute at all times and under all circumstances. There are certain well-defined and narrowly limited classes of speech, the prevention and punishment of which have never been thought to raise any Constitutional problem. These would include . . . the insulting or 'fighting words,' those which by their very utterance inflict injury or tend to incite an immediate breach of the peace."

Chaplinsky was further defined by *Gooding v Wilson* 1972 (Supreme Court). The "fighting words" must be in a face-to-face confrontation and lead to an immediate breach of the peace.

Village of Skokie v National Socialist Party 1978 (Illinois Supreme Court)

In 1976, the National Socialist Party planned to peacefully demonstrate in Skokie, Illinois, a community with a large Jewish population, to protest the racial integration of nearby Chicago schools. The protest was prohibited by village officials who said the Nazis failed to obtain $350,000 worth of liability and property damage insurance as required by a Skokie Park District ordinance quickly passed when the officials found out about the planned march. In addition, the village ruled that a member of a political party cannot march in a military-style uniform and ruled that it is not permissible to disseminate material intended to incite racial hatred.

State and federal courts in Illinois invalidated all the ordinances, ruling that they were discriminatory or abridged constitutionally protected rights of free speech. The Illinois Supreme Court rejected the contention that the display of such symbols as a swastika did not constitute "fighting words," sufficient to "overcome the heavy presumption against the constitutional validity of a prior restraint."

Peaceful demonstrations cannot be totally stopped or prohibited solely because they display (Nazi symbols) that may provoke a violent reaction by those who view them. A speaker who gives prior notice of his message has not compelled a confrontation with those who voluntarily listen.

R.A.V. v St. Paul 1992 (U.S. Supreme Court)

In 1982, St. Paul, Minnesota enacted a local hate-crime ordinance and created a new criminal offence: the bias motivated disorderly conduct crime. Under this ordinance, anyone who "places on public or private property, a symbol, object, appellation, characterization or graffiti" that "arouses anger, alarm or resentment in others on the basis of race, color, creed, or religion" was guilty of the misdemeanor offence of disorderly conduct. The city amended the law in 1989 to specifically include a burning cross or a Nazi swastika in the prohibitions, and in 1990 to prohibit actions based on sexual prejudice.

In 1990, Robert A. Viktora, a 17-year-old, reportedly a high school dropout and "skinhead," was joined by some other minors in placing a crude cross in the fenced yard of Russ and Laura Jones, the only Black family in a working-class neighborhood of St. Paul.

Court appointed attorney Edward J. Cleary, though not endorsing the youth's behavior, agreed to take the case because he, like many in Minnesota, felt that even though the actions were "despicable and deserved punishment" the law needed to be challenged on the basis that many felt it was overly restrictive of citizens' First Amendment rights.

On June 10, 1992, the case made its way to the Supreme Court.

On June 22, the Court overturned R.A.V.'s conviction in essence saying the St. Paul law was overly broad and overly restrictive.

Justice Antonin Scalia writing for the majority said: "Let there be no mistake about our belief that burning a cross in someone's yard is reprehensible. But St. Paul has sufficient means at its disposal to prevent such behavior without adding the First Amendment to the fire."

Scalia said that governments may not punish those who "communicate messages of racial, gender, or religious intolerance" merely because those ideas are offensive and emotionally painful to those in the targeted group.

The Court was unanimous in overturning the St. Paul hate speech ordinance, but they disagreed about the legal rationale for doing so. White, Blackman, Day-O'Connor, and Stevens argued that the ordinance was unconstitutional only because it was overly broad and not limited to expressions that could lead to violence under the "fighting words" test.

The other five justices joined the majority opinion in taking a much broader view of the First Amendment right of those who engage in "hate speech." They said that any law is unconstitutional if it singles out expression of "bias-motivated hatred" for special punishment. While the majority did not specifically overturn *Chaplinsky v New Hampshire*, they made it clear that the "fighting words" doctrine cannot ordinarily be used to suppress the expression of racial, religious, or gender-based hostilities.

The Court said that government must not single out expression on certain favored topics such as race and creed but not on others, such as homosexuality, union membership, or political affiliation.

Brandenburg v Ohio 1969 (U.S. Supreme Court)

The Supreme Court upheld the Klansman's right to make an offensive and bigoted speech at a Klan rally, as long as the speech did not create an imminent danger of violent acts.

Cohen v California 1971 (U.S. Supreme Court)

Paul R. Cohen, a 19-year-old department store worker, was criminally prosecuted for appearing in a Los Angeles County courthouse wearing a leather jacket bearing the motto "Fuck the Draft."

He was convicted of violating that part of California Penal Code 415 which prohibits "maliciously and willfully disturbing the peace or quiet of any neighborhood or person . . . by offensive conduct."

Justice John Marshall Harlan, writing for the majority, reversed the conviction:

"While the particular four-letter word being litigated here is perhaps more distasteful than most others of its genre, it is nevertheless often true that one man's vulgarity is another's lyric. Indeed, we think it is largely because governmental officials cannot make principled distinctions in this area that the Constitution leaves matters of taste and style so largely to the individual."

Texas v Johnson 491 1989 (U.S. Supreme Court)

Gregory Johnson and friends were arrested for violating a Texas law (Texas Penal Code, 42.09) that prohibited citizens from burning a state or national flag in a manner that offends . . . prohibited the desecration of a venerated object. Johnson and friends burned an American flag at the 1984 Republican National Convention in Dallas to protest the policies of President Ronald Reagan. He took the flag and lit it on fire on the steps of the convention center and he and others walked around the flag chanting "red, white, and blue, we spit on you." He was convicted and sentenced to one year in jail and fined $2,000. The Fifth District of Appeals in Dallas upheld the conviction. His attorney appealed Johnson's conviction to the U.S. Supreme Court on the basis that the Texas law was overly restrictive on his client's First Amendment rights.

In a 5-4 decision, the Court ruled that flag burning, especially in a political context, is a protected form of symbolic speech. The court noted that a "disturbing the peace" assertion was invalid. They also ruled that burning the flag would not fall under the "fighting words" exemption in the *Chaplinsky* case. Justice J. Kennedy said that no matter how distasteful the result, the First Amendment compelled it (the ruling) because the defendant's acts were speech in both the fundamental and technical sense.

Justice Brennan, writing for the majority, said:

"We are aware that desecration of the flag is deeply offensive to many. But the same might be said, for example, of virulent ethnic and religious epithets, vulgar repudiations of the draft, and scurrilous caricatures. There is a bedrock principle underlying the First Amendment, it is that the government may not prohibit the expression of an idea simply because society finds the idea itself offensive or disagreeable. Punishing desecration of the flag dilutes the very freedom that makes this emblem so revered and worth revering."

This Supreme Court decision proved very unpopular around the country. Many citizens expressed their anger over the fact that the Court had ruled that there were actually circumstances that might allow a person to desecrate that flag. These citizens wrote their respective Congressional representatives, which led to the passage of the **Flag Protection Act**, which made it a federal crime, punishable by one year in jail and a $1,000 fine, for desecrating the American flag.

After the Act became law, there were demonstrations across the nation. One of the new wave of flag burnings occurred on the steps of the national capitol building, resulting in four arrests and initiating the following test case.

United States v Eichman et al. 1990 (U.S. Supreme Court)

Shawn Eichman, a Revolutionary Communist Party member, along with other revolutionaries (including Mark John Haggerty and three others), staged a demonstration before a crowd of reporters and photographers. Witnesses reported hearing the defendants shout "burn, baby, burn" and "stop the Fascist flag law." The Supreme Court came back in the same 5–4 majority ruling the Flag Protection Act unconstitutional. Justice Brennan, writing for the majority, said:

U.S. District courts and U.S. Supreme Court reaffirmed the ruling in the *Texas v Johnson* case and added: *"Even assuming such a consensus (a national consensus supporting a ban on flag desecration as asserted by the government representatives in court) any suggestion that the governments' interest in suppressing speech becomes more weighty as popular opposition to that speech grows **is foreign to the First Amendment**.*

John Doe v University of Michigan 1989 (721 F. Supp. 852, 853)

In February of 1987, in response to incidents of racism and racial harassment on campus, the University of Michigan adopted a policy that prohibited "stigmatizing or victimizing individuals or groups on the basis of race, ethnicity, religion, sex, sexual orientation, creed, national origin, ancestry, age, marital status, handicap, or Vietnam-era status." In addition, the policy prohibited "such behavior if it involves an express or implied threat to or has the purpose or reasonably foreseeable effect of interfering with or creates an intimidating, hostile or demeaning environment for individual pursuits in academic, employment, or extracurricular activities."

John Doe was a Michigan psychology student who feared that discussion of certain theories about biological race and gender differences might be perceived as racist and sexist and therefore punishable under the campus policy.

The Federal District Court ruled the policy unconstitutional. The court said: "It is an unfortunate fact of our constitutional system that the ideals of freedom and equality are often in conflict."

Virginia v Black 2003 (U.S. Supreme Court)

In August of 1998, a 25-foot-high cross was burned at a rally of the Ku Klux Klan in Cana, Virginia. The burning was witnessed by a county sheriff and resulted in the arrest and prosecution of Barry Black for violation of Virginia Statute Section 18.2-423. The statute makes it a felony for any person to burn a cross with the intent to intimidate any person or group of persons; it also provides that cross burning constitutes a *prima facie* evidence of an intent to intimidate.

The Supreme Court of Virginia invalidated the conviction. The court relied on *v St. Paul*. In *R.A.V.*, the High Court ruled that a municipal cross-burning ordinance violated the First Amendment because the law improperly punished expression on the basis of the expression's content.

The Court reiterated that speech can be regulated only if it falls into well-defined categories: incitement constituting a clear and present danger to the government, commercial speech, fighting words that create an immediate danger of physical violence and obscenity and child pornography.

The Supreme Court held in *Black* that the operative language of the Virginia law, by specifically requiring an intent to intimidate and not including specified targets—on its surface—limited the law to true threats, which may be proscribed. A "true threat" is defined as one whereby the speaker "means to communicate a serious intention of an intent to commit an act of unlawful violence to an individual or group of individuals." This is not protected speech.

However, in *Black*, the court said that the addition of the provision for *prima facie* evidence, amounting as it did to a presumption of the intent to intimidate, rendered the statute unconstitutional on its face.

The jury that convicted Black had been told by the judge about the *prima facie* provision of the statute. On that basis, the court held Black's conviction to be improper because the *prima facie* provision removed any possibility that the act could be considered protected speech. Justice Sandra Day O'Connor wrote that the cross burning at the Klansmen meeting was not intended to threaten anyone present, it is communicative in nature; the *prima facie* provision ignores this distinction.

Study Guide Activities

Do an Online Search For:

Nichols v Chacon **1998**
110 F.Supp.2d 1099 (W. D. Ark, 2000).

Federal: An arrestee's display of his middle finger in an upward gesture, commonly referred to as "flipping someone off," "the bird," or "giving someone the finger," did not constitute "fighting words" and, thus, was protected as free speech under the First Amendment in a civil rights action brought under 42 U.S.C. sec. 1983. The court ruled that the arresting police officer was not entitled to qualified immunity in the lawsuit. It said the arrestee-plaintiff's gesture was clearly established as protected, free speech at the time when the officer issued a ticket to the arrestee for disorderly conduct.

"While we agree the gesture utilized by Nichols was crude, insensitive, offensive, and disturbing to Chacon's sensibilities, it was not obscene under the relevant Supreme Court precedent, did not constitute 'fighting words,' and was protected as 'free speech' under the First Amendment to the United States Constitution. We also believe that this right was clearly established on August 6th of 1998 when Chacon arrested Nichols.

Accordingly, we hold as a matter of law that Chacon is not entitled to qualified immunity and that his arrest of Nichols violated Nichols' First and Fourth Amendment rights."

Snyder V Phelps **2011 (U.S. Supreme Court)**
Westboro Baptist Church—Note the courts majority ruling in this case. The church is infamous for their protests expressing hatred for gay persons in the military, often picketing military funerals because they feel America's growing acceptance of homosexuals stems firstly from the military.

38 | Chapter 8 Talk Is Cheap—Free Speech Is Not

What did the lower courts award? What did the Fourth Circuit Court rule? What ultimately did SCOTUS rule? Also, who were the defendant's attorneys?

Do an online search on "freedom of expression." List the top five sites you found.

Read and find out if the sites you listed mention any of the court cases in this lesson.

Do an online search on the *Virginia v Black* case. Summarize the dissenting opinion in the case.

Absence of Malice

Chapter 9

This video can be shown in special class sessions or rented by students individually to point out the importance of the *New York Times Co. v Sullivan* Supreme Court case. This film supports lectures on media law, ethics, and methodology.

An ambitious young reporter (Sally Field as Megan) exhibits the traits of an overzealous reporter out to "get the scoop" and get it first. We find that any means justify that end. The storyline also explores the ethics of the federal government in achieving its "ends" in an investigation into the death of a local union member.

The movie shows how a private businessman, Michael Gallagher (Paul Newman), can be unknowingly drawn into a tangled web of questionable ethical behavior and learn how powerless we are when confronted with the powers of the press and government.

Issues related to the movie to be discussed and/or covered on exams:

- Powers of the FBI (executive branch of the federal government)
- Fourth Amendment—Invasion of privacy (by both the newspaper and the federal government)
- First Amendment's guarantee of the "public's right to know"
- Shield laws
- Right to print defamatory information if "to the best of your knowledge, the information is true," after convincing yourself that you have been "reasonable and prudent" in your investigation to make sure you are not negligent
- Power of the Fourth Estate to print what they want
- Illegal searches and seizures, trespass, search warrants
- What constitutes a credible source for a story in the paper?
- Do newspapers print only the TRUTH?
- What is the process gatekeepers use to decide what does or does not go in the newspaper?
- Does the fact that you print private information about a person make them more credible as a source for a story?
- What rights do public figures and public officials have?
- Listen carefully to what James J. Wells from the U.S. Department of Justice has to say at the end of the movie. How does he sum up the roles of government and newspapers?
- What ultimately happens to the characters of Quinn and Rosen in the movie? Why do they end up the way they do?

Absence of Malice is a Sydney Pollack film released in 1981. Runs 117 minutes.

Student Notes

Newspapers

Chapter 10

In 1776, the Continental Congress adopted the Declaration of Independence; the text of the document was published in the *Pennsylvania Evening Post* of July 6. The next year, the Continental Congress authorized Mary Katherine Goddard, publisher of the *Maryland Journal*, to print the first official copies of the Declaration with the names of the signers attached.

Four Elements of News

1. Impact
2. Proximity
3. Timeliness
4. Credibility

Gatekeepers for the print and broadcast media use these guidelines to determine, in priority order, what goes into their respective news reports.

The most important story on the front page usually appears in the upper right side of the front page in more traditionally designed newspapers. The reason for this is that the reader looks at the paper nameplate and their eye drops to that spot. Editors use print font size, style, and number of decks in headlines to lead readers through the front page of their newspaper. Serif typeface is the easiest to read. Sans serif may look cleaner and more modern and is usually used in headlines and news graphics.

In Orange County, we have two competing newspapers with very different philosophies on design. The *Los Angeles Times* (*L.A. Times*) is more traditional in its news layout, while the *Orange County Register* (*O.C. Register*) is more likely to experiment with more modern design features. *O.C. Register* was noted for its early use of color in its newspaper, winning a Pulitzer Prize for its color photography of the 1984 Los Angeles Olympic Games.

States.

Visit the website given below to see newspaper front pages across the United
http://www.newseum.org/todaysfrontpages/flash/

Chapter 10 Newspapers

Study Guide Questions

Contact an editor of a local paper and ask them their policy on:

- Use of anonymous sources
- Policy on freebies
- Policy on junkets
- Impact

Some gatekeepers say, "Seems that life threatening situations have the most impact in our society." What are some of these situations and why do they make front-page news?

Many professional writers say, "Those who can write will be worth their weight in gold." Why so? What do you think?

Discuss editorial pages' design and philosophy. What elements are in the paper's nameplate and what does that tell the reader, right away, about the paper?

Consult your text and/or do an online search for the following and be prepared to identify them on an exam:

- Johann Gutenberg
- *Publick Occurrences both Forreign and Domestick*, 1690 Benjamin Harris
- *New England Courant*, James Franklin
- *Pennsylvania Gazette*, Ben Franklin
- John Peter Zenger
- What was the impact of the early colonial press?
- Penny Press
- Horace Greeley
- Yellow Journalism—where did we get the term?
- Newspaper Wars in New York Between Joseph Pulitzer (*St Louis Post-Dispatch*) (*New York World*) and William Randolph Hearst (*San Francisco Examiner*) (*New York Journal*)
- Muckrakers
- Henry Luce

Chapter 10 Newspapers | **43**

USA Today
Minority Newspapers
Declining Competition in the Newspaper Industry
Impact of Blogs on Newspaper Circulation (web log)
Impact of online sites like Craigslist on newspapers.

What do you feel is the future of newspapers in the United States and the world?

List some tabloid newspapers in your region.

List some of the special sections newspapers are adding to reach a wider audience.

Student Notes

Chapter 11

Media Ownership

Media Consolidation

- Convergence: Sometimes called media convergence (though this term has several meanings)
- Definition: It describes the process by which several media outlets (film and television studios, newspapers, magazines, websites, etc.) are purchased by one of a small handful of organizations
- Mergers: Many major organizations, like AT&T decide to merge (like AOL Time Warner or Universal NBC)

Five companies own everything. That might seem like an exaggeration, but in the media industry, the Big 5 (it was the Big 6 until Disney bought several Fox properties in 2017) run almost everything under the sun. Have doubts? See if any of your favorite things are owned by the few. Consider these names:

- Bain Capital/Thomas H. Lee Partners (Clear Channel)
- CBS Corporation
- Comcast Corporation
- Gannett Co.
- News Corp
- Time Warner, Inc.
- Tribune Company
- Viacom
- Walt Disney Company
- Washington Post Company

There are small success stories of media ownership, like the news blog by Andrew Sullivan, a former editor for The New Republic, who thrived and payed a small staff solely based on profits from voluntary subscriptions. But for the most part, economics prevent some organizations from functioning the way they hope.

Meet the Big 6

- Comcast $80.4 billion
- The Walt Disney Company $55.6 billion

45

- Time Warner $28.1 billion
- 20th Century Fox $27.3 billion
- CBS $13.8 billion
- Viacom $12.4 billion

*Separate but still subsidiaries of National Amusements
*Money is revenue from 2016.

News Corp used to be the banner company for Fox, but a split occurred between news holdings and broadcast/film content.

The Big 6 will soon become known as the Big 5, however, after Disney purchased entertainment holdings from 20th Century Fox in 2017. Now, Disney owns networks and studios like FOX, FX, FXX, 20th Century Fox, and Fox Searchlight, along with its own properties like Buena Vista, Pixar, Marvel Studios, ABC, Freeform, and ESPN.

Working Together

- Media ownership is often complicated. For example, The CW is owned by Time Warner and CBS following the merger of two networks, The WB and UPN.
- Companies share the financial load; a TV series like *Gotham* is produced by Warner Bros. and sold to FOX, who airs it.
- Sometimes this process becomes complicated. *The Dark Tower*, a box-office flop, had input from distributer Columbia Pictures, production company MRC, and director Nikolaj Arcel (many claim this is why is flopped). Since no one would cede on many points, the result was a film that didn't performance well at the box office.

Notable Big Wigs

- Sony Pictures ($8.3B): Columbia Pictures, TriStar Pictures, Screen Gems, Sony Pictures Classics, MGM
- iHeartMedia ($6.2B): Previously Clear Channel, iHeartRadio, owned by Bain Capital and Thomas H. Lee Partners
- Netflix ($8.8B): Labeled an internet company, known for making deals with other networks and tech brands (Hulu only earned $1 billion in 2013)

Concentrated Power

- Look up how the MTV show Skins was canceled (it was over moral reasons)
- Who controls (funds) the narrative?
- Who watches the watchmen?
- And what happens when those watchmen are funded by those they seek to critique?
- What does information diversity mean when six companies own everything?

Try an experiment during the week: download major news apps (Fox, ABC, CBS, NBC, AP, USA Today, CNN, etc.), activate notifications and track what each app considers worthy of immediate release.

Billionaires Who Own the News

- Rupert Murdoch: Fox News, *The Wall Street Journal*, *New York Post*, *Sky News*, and HarperCollins
- Don & Sam Newhouses: *Wired, Vanity Fair, Vogue, Glamour, GQ, Self, Allure, Bon Appetit*, and more than 60 newspapers
- Jeff Bezos: Amazon CEO bought *The Washington Post*
- John Henry: Red Sox owner bought *The Boston Globe*
- Sheldon Adelson: *Las Vegas Review-Journal* (purchased secretly through his son-in-law)
- Patrick Soon-Shiong: Tribune Publishing, including the *Los Angeles Times* and the *Chicago Tribune*

Major Organizations & the News

- Time Warner: CNN, Time, *People, InStyle, Real Simple, Entertainment Weekly, Sports Illustrated, Essence, LIFE, Homes & Gardens,* and *Southern Living*
- Disney: ABC News, ESPN, some TV stations
- CBS: CBS News, multiple TV stations, KNX 1070, KROQ 106.7
- Comcast: NBC News, MSNBC, CNBC, The Weather Channel, E!, Rotten Tomatoes
- News Corp: Fox News, *The Wall Street Journal*, *New York Post*
- Viacom: The Daily Show, MTV, VH1

The Big 6 have mostly lost interest in traditional print media (though Time Warner cares about magazines). What does that mean?

Background on the *L.A. Times*

The history of the *L.A. Times* can really be directly linked to the past and present development of Southern California.

Harrison Gray Otis

Harris Gray Otis was born on February 10, 1837 in Marietta, Ohio. His parents were named Stephen and Sarah Otis. He was the youngest of 16 siblings. His uncle was a senator from Massachusetts. He worked on the family farm and went to school during the three months of winter.

- At age 14, he became a printer's apprentice for the *Noble County Courier* in Ohio.
- In 1859, he married Eliza A. Wetherby and established a home in Louisville, Kentucky.
- At age 23, Otis was elected a member of the 1860 Republican National Convention that nominated Abraham Lincoln.

- Otis and Eliza left Kentucky for Ohio where he enlisted as a private in the Twelfth Regiment of the Ohio Volunteer Infantry at Camp Dennison, Ohio, June 25, 1861 to fight on the side of the North in the Civil War. He fought in 15 battles and was wounded twice. He received four promotions and two brevets to major and lieutenant colonel. He was cited for gallant service.
- He worked as a Washington correspondent for the *Ohio State Journal*. He was once the managing editor of the *Grand Army Journal*, the first Union soldiers' paper established in Washington after the war.
- He came to California in 1876. On March 11, 1876, Otis took control of the *Santa Barbara Press* newspaper, which he published for four years. He came to Los Angeles when he learned that the newest newspaper, the *L.A. Daily Times*, was for sale. In 1882, he bought a quarter interest in the *Times*. He became the editor for the *Times* as well the *Los Angeles Mirror*. He made $15 a week. Wife Eliza also contributed articles about women, religion, and morals to the paper.
- In 1882, Los Angeles was a dirty dusty town with a population of 5,000. In 1883, the Southern Pacific Railroad came to California with a spur to Los Angeles.
- In 1883, Otis and H.H. Boyce became co-owners of the *Times*, which had grown to eight pages. They established the Times Mirror Company. The paper printed articles about how great the climate was in Southern California.
- Otis later bought Boyce out. Boyce started the *Morning Tribune*. After which there were two morning papers: the *Times* and the *Tribune*. There was one afternoon paper: William Randolph Hearst's the *Herald and Express*.
- In 1884, one year after the Southern Pacific Railroad came to Los Angeles; the city's population was 12,000.
- In 1886, Los Angeles's population was 100,000. The Southern Pacific and the Atchison, Topeka, and Santa Fe railroads engaged in a fare war. The fare from Kansas City to Los Angeles was $1. During 1886, the volume of newspaper real estate advertising reached a figure of $100,000,000.

Harry Chandler

Harry Chandler was 27 years younger than Otis. He moved to Hollywood at age 17 (worth $500 million when he died in 1944). He suffered from pneumonia as a result of a fraternity initiation at Dartmouth College at age 17. The family doctor recommended he go to Southern California. Chandler made $19 a day hauling fruit to the central valley. He saved $3000 in two years.

- Chandler was able to gain control of the circulation (1,400 persons) list of the *Times*; he also gained control of the lists for the afternoon *Herald* and the morning *Tribune* newspapers as well. Through his control of the lists, he was able to help put the *Tribune* out of business. Within two years, he was able to put Otis's main competitor (Boyce) out of business. When the *Tribune* folded in 1890, Harry Chandler reportedly sent a third party to buy the *Tribune*'s production equipment for about five cents to the dollar. After Boyce went out of business, *Times* circulation and advertising quadrupled.
- In 1888, Chandler and Otis started the Los Angeles Chamber of Commerce. In 1894, Chandler married Otis's daughter Marian. Harry and Marian had eight children, the oldest son

was Norman. In 1897, The Los Angeles Merchant and Manufacturers Association formed, led by the *L.A. Times*.

- In 1890s, Los Angeles needed a natural port. The *Times* lobbied to have the harbor built in San Pedro over the push by the principals of the Southern Pacific Railroad to have it built in Santa Monica. The organization's main objective was to keep organized labor out of Los Angeles.
- Labor strife from 1907 to 1910. The *Times* building was bombed October 1, 1910. Twenty were killed, 21 were injured. Clarence Darrow defended the culprits, the McNamara brothers.
- In 1902, the federal government with the support of Teddy Roosevelt passed the Land Reclamation Act. The executive branch set up the Bureau of Land Management.
- J.B. Lippincott and engineer J.C. Clausen, hired by the government, traveled to the Owens Valley to get the land owners to give up their water rights. At about the same time, Fred Eaton and William Mulholland went to the Owens Valley and started to purchase controlling land holdings along the river.
- At about the same time in Los Angeles, Otis, Chandler, and others formed the San Fernando Mission Land Company and started buying up cheap land in the San Fernando Valley. M.H. Sherman and Henry Huntington (prominent names in Los Angeles today) were also involved.
- The media had learned that the city was working to lock up water rights 259 miles to the north in the Owens Valley. Mulholland was working to develop a monumental plan to build an aqueduct to bring that water all the way to Los Angeles. The Los Angeles Metropolitan Water District got control of key parcels in the valley without those living there knowing the ultimate fate of their land and water in the valley. Then, with the help of the federal government and a bond issue drive led by the *Times*, the aqueduct was begun.
- On July 28, 1905, the *Times* broke the news that Owens River water would be coming 235 miles to Los Angeles. The *L.A. Times* editorialized to pass the $20 million-plus bond to build the aqueduct.
- Options and land purchases the Chandlers and others on the inside made jumped in value. Options on land purchased or optioned by the Mission Valley Land Co. reportedly increased 100-fold.
- Harrison Gray Otis died on July 30, 1917; he was 80 years old.
- Norman and Harry Chandler were instrumental in persuading Donald Douglas to relocate his aircraft building business to Los Angeles. They also played a role in the relocation of the film making industry to Los Angeles.
- Los Angeles lacked a natural harbor like San Francisco and San Diego. So, the Chandlers led a drive to bring a harbor to Los Angeles and they were instrumental in the harbor being built in Long Beach instead of Santa Monica. Collis P. Huntington of the Southern Pacific Railroad always thought the natural spot for a harbor would be Santa Monica. The Atchison, Topeka, and Santa Fe wanted it built at Redondo Beach. Norman was on the board of the Santa Fe Railroad and the Chandlers had bought some of the best properties in the San Pedro port area.
- Dorothy Buffum raised $19 million to save the Hollywood Bowl. Norman and Buff had two children, Otis and Camilla. Norman died in 1973 of throat cancer. The children paddled past the surf in Dana Point to spread his ashes.

Otis Chandler

Otis Chandler fell from horse at age seven. His mother took him to more than one hospital to find one that would ultimately save the boy's life. He was a Stanford athlete, a shot putter of Olympic caliber.

- In 1953, he was discharged from the Air Force. He and his wife Missy had two children at the time.
- Upon joining the staff of the *Times*, he was presented with a seven-page memo outlining steps for working his way through the *Times* from press room to publisher.
- He was credited with bringing the *Times* to a position of national and international prominence. He died in 2006 of Lewy body disease, a brain disorder combining some of the most debilitating characteristics of Parkinson's and Alzheimer's diseases.

Study Guide Questions

Did the owners of the *L.A. Times* make their fortunes solely on the publishing of a newspaper? Explain.

What advantage did the owners of the *Times*, the largest circulating newspaper in the region, have through the ability to "select" the news and set agendas through their editorial pages?

In what ways do you feel the ownership of a major news outlet allowed the owners to shape the development of a geographic region? This could be true in New York, Florida, the Midwest, the South and of course, the West Coast.

Through an online search give the ownership and editorial status of the *L.A. Times* today.

How has the addition of many more media outlets, including television, radio and many more newspapers and magazines, impacted the power of the *L.A. Times*?

Chapter 11   Media Ownership | 51

What is the impact of the Internet on newspapers today? Think Craigslist

What do you feel is the future of the printed newspaper?

How do you access news?

Student Notes

Radio/Radio and Politics

Chapter 12

In the early days of radio development, individuals built their own crystal radio sets in their own homes. A few of the fledgling stations began experimenting with entertainment programs.

One of the early station owners who used radio to acquire wealth and influence was William S. Paley, founder of the modern-day Columbia Broadcast System (CBS). Paley's grandfather was a Russian who owned a lumber mill outside of Kiev. He found that many of his Jewish friends and neighbors were the subject of discrimination and persecution. Issac Paley sensed the danger and took a trip to the United States. He liked what he saw there and came back to get his family, sell the lumber mill, and leave in 1884 for the United States. The family settled in Chicago.

Soon his sons, Sam and Jake, developed a talent for blending tobacco and sold cigars from a pushcart on the streets. The cigars were so popular that they formed the Congress Cigar Company.

Young Bill Paley (born in 1901), Sam's son, soon was attending college and working summers in the cigar factory. It was Bill, who first ran a radio advertisement for the company on WCAU Philadelphia. For $50 a week, the company got a ten-piece orchestra and a singer. They called the entertainment the "Miss La Palina" show. When Jake noticed the expenditure, he ordered young Bill to discontinue the program. Jake saw the advertising on radio as frivolous at best. However, after taking the program off the radio waves, Sam was confronted around town about why the program left the air. The company had been running print advertising for years and people did not stop him on the street to discuss the issue. Plus, after another check of the books, Sam noticed that sales had gone up with the radio advertising. Here he was confronted daily about what happened to the radio show. Soon young Bill was exonerated and the show was resumed.

To shorten the story, Sam and Jake sold the Congress Cigar Company for around $30 million right before the Great Depression to Dillon, Read & Co.

It was around this time that young Bill noticed that a fledgling radio station with a first floor office in New York City was for sale. In 1928, he bought CBS for $400,000 (with Sam and Jake's help).

The first year, CBS posted gross earnings of $1.4 million. By the third year, the company posted earnings of $4.7 million. By 1937, CBS reported earnings of 27.7 million and it owned 114 stations.

Key concept that led to CBS's profitability: Paley came up with the idea of giving his programming away for free to any stations that wanted it. In return he asked only a guarantee that if he wanted to preempt a certain time slot, the station would have to make it available to him, either for free or for a reasonable fee. This allowed his company to go to advertisers and guarantee them a huge audience at specified prime times across the nation. In other words, instead of selling the programs to the stations and having them raise the money in their own communities to pay for it,

Paley gave the programs away in exchange for large audiences in prime time. Thus, he was able to offer national exposure for a company's product.

IT WORKED! That, along with his natural sense of what the general American public thought was entertaining led to CBS's success. Some of the more popular radio personalities and shows: Bing Crosby, Will Rogers, Frank Sinatra, Jack Benny, Amos n Andy, George Burns, Red Skelton, Edward Murrow.

Radio and Politics

Franklin Delano Roosevelt (FDR) is a prime example of personal/political public relations.

Across the nation, from the time of the nation's founding, very few American citizens had actually seen the president in person. For more than 150 years, they had seen pictures in print publications and read news stories about the president as related in the nation's print publications but very few had ever seen or heard the president's voice.

When FDR went live on radio with his fireside chats, the impact on the country was tremendous. Now people across the country could sit in their living rooms and listen to the president speak to them about the state of the nation and during time of war he was able to reassure them and keep them abreast of his efforts to lead the country.

In 1933, President Herbert Hoover had one person handling about 40 letters a day to the president. After the fireside chats began, FDR was receiving more than 4,000 letters a day. Stores could not keep up with the consumer demand for radios. FDR already had a special relationship with most of the print media and he was not self assured about going live on radio but he was a natural. He possessed a deep, resonant voice and his slower speech lent a sense of calm and confidence. People across the nation from that generation still remember the name of FDR's dog Fala as the dog often sat beside him during his fireside chats. As many as 50 million Americans were regularly listening to the broadcasts.

FDR died in his fourth term in office. The popularity he enjoyed with the American public was much attributed to his use of and understanding of the media both print and electronic. This led our elected representatives in Congress to initiate and later ratify the Twenty-Second Amendment to the U.S. Constitution.

Twenty-Second Amendment to the U.S. Constitution
(Ratified February 27, 1951)

Section 1. No person shall be elected to the office of the President more than twice, and no person who has held the office of President, or acted as President, for more than two years of a term to which some other person was elected President shall be elected to the office of the President more than once. But this Article shall not apply to any person holding the office of President when this Article was proposed by the Congress, and shall not prevent any person who may be holding the office of President, or acting as President, during the term within which this Article becomes operative from holding the office of President acting as President during the remainder of such term.

Section 2. This article shall be inoperative unless it shall have been ratified as an amendment to the Constitution by the legislatures of three-fourths of the several States within seven years from the date of its submission to the States by the Congress.

Chapter 12 Radio/Radio and Politics | 55

Names and terms needed for transfer to four-year colleges/universities.

Possible exam questions requiring text, online, library, and other research for exam questions:

Lee de Forest

Reginald Fessenden

David Sarnoff

Guglielmo Marconi

Heinrich Hertz

Radio Act of 1927

Federal Communications Commission

Telecommunications Act of 1996

National Public Radio

Arbitron

Amplitude Modulation (AM)

Equal Time/ Equal Opportunities Doctrine

Fairness Doctrine

Chapter 12 Radio/Radio and Politics

Study Guide Questions

List at least four radio talk shows available in your area.

What seems to be their agenda other than to make lots of money?
According to Newsweek, Nov. 2010
Rush Limbaugh ($58.7 million annually)
Glenn Beck ($33 million annually)
Sean Hannity ($22 million annually)
Search for updated data and see if you can add other TV personalities to the list.

Do you feel that the strategy of some talk show hosts is to create an atmosphere of Fear, Anger, and Hate just to generate rating?

Listen to one or more daytime talk shows.
Do they offer air time to qualified persons with opposing points of view? If yes, why? If no, why?

After listening to a couple of the most popular talk shows, relate their agenda to what you found out about the Equal times/Equal opportunities provision and the Fairness Doctrine in the 1934 Federal Communications Act.

Television Programming

Chapter 13

James T. Aubrey

CBS, under Bill Paley's leadership, moved from radio broadcast prominence to television success. One of the early popular shows was *The $64,000 Question*. When it was learned that the program directors had "fixed" the show, CBS lost credibility. Paley had to do something and he fired his, then, president of the television network, Lou Cowan.

Paley replaced Cowan with an up and coming television program director, James Aubrey.

When Aubrey took over in December of 1959, CBS profits were about $25.2 million. When Aubrey was fired by Paley in 1964, profits were $48.6 million. Aubrey was said to have a "killer instinct" for the lowest common denominator. He was a master at providing the least objectionable programming. A *Life* magazine article about him after his fall from CBS said, "No man in history ever had such a lock on such enormous audiences."

His formula: Rural comedies, detective stories, the 3 Bs (broads, boobs, and busts), no old people acting old, no physical infirmities, NO SOCIAL ISSUES, no maids.

Aubrey wanted programs that required as little thinking as possible. He demanded happy endings. His programs: *The Beverly Hillbillies, Mr. Ed, Green Acres, Petticoat Junction, The Munsters, 77 Sunset Strip* (while at ABC), *Gunsmoke, Have Gun—Will Travel, The Red Skelton Show, Father Knows Best, Wanted: Dead or Alive, Perry Mason, Route 66, Barbra Streisand specials, The Wild, Wild West, The Danny Kaye Show* (a variety show).

Other interesting notes regarding Aubrey:

- Nicknamed "the Smiling Cobra" by John Houseman.
- He was the most press-shy (if not the most written about) of modern show business executives.
- Treated his boss, Bill Paley, with disdain.
- Aubrey was the man, the monarch, on the 20th floor of CBS at a time in the early 1960s when CBS could be compared to JFK's Camelot. (It was Paley's company but Aubrey's network, the saying went.)
- The bottom line: In 1963, CBS under Aubrey had 12 of the top 15 night-time series and all 12 of the top 12 daytime series.
- Aubrey interview quote: "Jack Kennedy was a friend of mine," Aubrey mused late on a recent Saturday. "We used to talk about this whole thing of being 'ladies' men.' People

thought we got away with a lot more than we really did ... I'm certainly no example of clean living. But as I always said, 'If a man can be indicted for liking pretty girls, I'm guilty.'"

- Aubrey once expressed what he felt was the thing that separates the men from the boys. "In my opinion, the one thing in terms of leadership that stands out, is not intelligence or ability. Those who operate most effectively, those I respect most, simply are not afraid. And most people are afraid, they're scared of decisions."
- Aubrey played end on the Princeton football team in 1938.

Students must do an online search to get more information on James T. Aubrey.

Study Guide Activities and Issues

Possible exam essay: Compare and contrast James T. Aubrey's formula for television programming success with television programs today.

Please see the study guide chapter on "New Media" for latest developments in TV viewing options which have impacted TV viewer's habits and TV programming.

Through online, text, and other research methods, identify:

Vladimir Zworykin

David Sarnoff (as relates specifically to television)

When and where was television first introduced to the American people?

Milton Berle

Philo Farnsworth

Nielsen: What is a television program's rating? Share?

People Meters

Sweeps (four times a year)

Zippers, Zappers, Flippers, TiVo, VCR and now DVR viewer's habits.

Do you feel that some television "news" programs set an agenda rather that just report the news and let you analyze the information?

What news sources do you trust the most?

Student Notes

Television and Politics

Chapter 14

The electronic media has transformed politics in the United States. As pointed out in a previous unit of study, the impact of radio was immense. Most of the nation had participated in the democratic process having never heard or seen the president other than in the print media.

In the minds of many media scholars, television changed politics forever in the 1952 presidential campaign between Dwight David (Ike) Eisenhower and Adlai Stevenson. It is interesting to note that the candidates were approached by CBS's Bill Paley about the possibility of a nation-wide television debate between the candidates. Eisenhower's television consultant, David Schoenbrun, turned down the invitation.

Efforts were made to make Ike more TV friendly. He was asked to change his military-like bearing. Instead of chin in, chest out, he was advised to lift his head and relax his shoulders and chest thus showing more cheekbone than bald head. He was also approached about the use of makeup to dull the facial glair presented by the lighting necessary in early television technology. Ike was the first presidential candidate to use one-minute television commercials. He was also, with the help of Paley, the first presidential candidate to announce his candidacy live on television. Later, after he was elected, Ike became the first president to be broadcast live from the White House on TV.

The 1952, Republican convention was also notable because Richard Nixon, the vice presidential nominee, was accused of some improper use of campaign funds and he went live on television to refute the charges. The famous "Checkers speech," (Checkers being Nixon's dog which he said was the only gift he and his wife Pat had accepted as related to the campaign) was viewed by thousands and Nixon's words and demeanor swayed the American people and the Republican party to stay with his vice presidential nomination.

Writes:

In a 1982 book by George Ball, titled *The Past Has Another Pattern*, the author

> "Stevenson would, I knew be repelled by the idea of using thirty second, or even one minute spots with only a scattered handful of nationally televised half-hour speeches. He still sincerely believed that a campaign should be used to educate people, not narcotize them by an endless succession of asinine political commercials. Spots could not convey ideas, only create fleeting artificial impressions, thus putting a premium on manner and personality. 'Sooner or later' I predicted in an informal speech in New York: 'Presidential campaigns would have professional actors as candidates who could speak the lines.' I did not know how presciently I spoke."

Chapter 14 Television and Politics

At the 1952 Republican convention, Walter Cronkite and Edward R. Morrow were anchoring the television broadcast. They were setting new standards for political coverage in America. They found it difficult to ask their questions from up in the control booth and their man on the floor had to compete with legions of print media reporters.

While Nixon was being questioned about campaign contributions on the floor of the convention by print-media reporters, the television anchors in the control booth reportedly told their representative on the floor holding a microphone to put his earphones on Nixon. He did as he was told and Nixon was now listening only to the questions posed by Cronkite and Murrow and the print reporters were just standing around staring.

Most political science courses, when dealing with the impact of television on politics, focus on the famous 1960 debates between Richard Nixon and John F. Kennedy.

There were four debates. Kennedy is credited with legitimizing television and polling systems for presidential politics. Kennedy's father used family money to hire Lou Harris who developed a system for finding out the values and needs of the electorate and helping Kennedy's speech writers address those issues.

Books and other print media relate that the Kennedy camp arrived in Chicago a week early for the debates realizing how important they could be. Nixon on the other hand shunned the advice of his media guru Ted Rogers and stayed on the campaign trail until hours before that first debate. There were issues regarding use of makeup that can be researched.

Those who listened to the debate on radio felt Nixon came out on top. However, those viewing the debate overwhelmingly chose Kennedy as the winner. The importance of "reaction shots" in the first televised debate was an important part of the later evaluation of the impact of the TV debate.

It is interesting to note that surveys and forums have found that three quarters of the American people believe that the press has a negative impact on the presidential campaigns with many adding that television campaign coverage leads candidates to perform for the cameras rather than focus on issues.

Study Guide Questions

Does a relentless negativism, enhanced by the criticism in ad campaigns, lead to a public perception that the race is much more negative than political observers think?

Do you feel the media may be able to shape public discourse? Does the media set the agenda for public discussion, whether intentionally or unintentionally? Important issues presented by the media include but are not limited to: color of ties; personalities of the wives and the wives' haircuts, clothes, makeup; balloons falling to the floor at the convention. CNN recently hired a comedian to find "entertaining" sidebars at the convention. America is not ready for some serious political discourse according to their news producers. The gatekeepers pick the issues and sound bites to feed to the large, anonymous, heterogeneous mass of receivers.

Does the candidate who can shape the mediated political discourse, who can control the issues of the campaign through careful media manipulation, win the race?

Do the media fixate on who is winning and losing instead of what the candidates are proposing?

Do political ads define the nature of the presidency by stipulating the attributes a president should have?

Is it difficult for the average American to rely on news to correct or balance political advertisements when Americans are more exposed to and conditioned to advertising formats?

Media corporations are high-powered businesses in a highly competitive capitalistic economic system. They have always sought the unusual, the titillating, and the sensational.

Are today's media outlets becoming less balanced? If less balanced, is this polarization of news coverage reflective of a more politically polarized society?

Should the media, even though in competition for corporate profits, hold themselves to a higher standard of credibility?

In 2013 Newsweek listed the annual income of top television personalities: Glenn Beck, $33 million, Sean Hannity, $22 million, Bill O'Reilly, $20 million Jon Stewart, $15 million, Laura Ingraham, $7 million,

Student Notes

Obscenity and Pornography

Chapter 15

Lecture and Notes

The impact of sexually explicit material in our society is debated daily. During the 1960s, a presidential commission was formed to explore the dangers of pornography and later in the 1980s another panel was convened to determine the nature and extent of the effects of obscenity and pornography in the United States. Here is a brief outline of court cases that will help you to explore the issue from an academic point of view:

Of special note will be our discussion of the findings of both the 1960 study done under President Lyndon Johnson and the 1986 Meese Commission report under President Ronald Reagan.

Tariff Act of 1842

This Act prohibited the importation of all indecent and obscene prints, paintings, lithographs, and engravings. It was later expanded in 1857 to include written material.

Regina v Hicklin 1868

QB (Queens Bench) 360 bans all material that tends to deprave and corrupt those whose minds are open to immoral influence. This case traces attempts to censor sexually explicit material back to England. The Hicklin test: "whether the tendency of the matter charged as obscene is to deprave and corrupt those whose minds are open to such immoral influences and into whose hands a publication of this sort might fall."

Of note is the fact that many felt that an entire publication could be considered obscene if any portion could deprave and/or corrupt.

Federal Anti-Obscenity Act 1873

Ban from the mail all obscene, lewd, lascivious or filthy books, pamphlets, pictures, papers, letter writing ... Known as the Comstock Law for Anthony Comstock, the federal agent charged with ferreting out immoral materials.

Prurient (Latin root): To itch, to yearn for, to be lascivious, arouses an obsessive or morbid interest in sex.

Roth v United States 1957

Samuel Roth convicted for violating federal obscenity statutes barring the mailing of obscene materials.

The Supreme Court ruled that a work is obscene if:

- the dominant theme of the material taken as a whole appeals to a prurient interest in sex,
- the material is patently offensive because it affronts contemporary community standards relating to the description or representation of sexual matters,
- the material is utterly without redeeming social value.

Memoirs v Massachusetts 1966

Memoirs of a Woman of Pleasure (Fannie Hill)

The eighteenth-century novel by John Cleland included many sexually explicit passages. Supreme Court reaffirmed the Roth ruling and went on to say that if the work had any redeeming social value, no matter how minimal, it is protected by First Amendment. Lower courts convicted. Supreme Court reversed.

Stanley v Georgia 1969

Robert Eli Stanley was convicted of violating Georgia state laws regarding the possession of obscene materials in one's own home. Stanley was suspected of running a betting operation in his home; the police, while searching his residence, found three reels of pornographic films.

Justice Thurgood Marshal, writing for the majority, said:

"If the First Amendment means anything, it means that a state has no business telling a man sitting alone in his own house what book he may read or films he may watch. Our whole constitutional heritage rebels at the thought of giving government the power to control men's minds."

Miller v California 1973

California courts found Marvin Miller guilty of sending unsolicited obscene advertising through the mail in violation of state law.

In this case the Supreme Court reaffirmed that obscenity is not protected by the First Amendment but went on to give state legislatures better guidelines regarding what may be legally obscene.

A work is obscene if:

- "the average person, applying contemporary community standards" would find that the work, taken as a whole, appeals to the prurient interest . . .
- the work depicts or describes, in a patently offensive way, sexual conduct specifically defined by the applicable state law.
- the work, taken as a whole, lacks serious literary, artistic, political, or scientific value.

Chief Justice Warren Burger also included some definitions of what may be "patently offensive."

1960s Commission on Obscenity and Pornography
Democratic President Lyndon Johnson

- Three years and $2 million to study the "puzzle of pornography"
- Basically the commission found no link between viewing sexually explicit material and subsequent anti-social behavior.

Findings will be discussed in class. Do a computer search on the results of this study.

1980s The Meese Commission

President Ronald Reagan's attorney general Edwin Meese convened a panel of 11 people, most of them prominent conservatives:

"to determine the nature, extent, and impact on society of pornography in the United States and to make specific recommendations to the Attorney General concerning more effective ways to which the spread of pornography could be contained consistent with constitutional guarantees."

- The study found a direct relationship between viewing sexually explicit material depicting violence and aggressive behavior toward women and incidents of the same behavior toward women.
- The commission found a link between viewing sexually explicit materials depicting women in situations of degradation, subordination, domination, or humiliation and the incidence of different nonviolent forms of discrimination against or subordination of women in our society.

Ashcroft v the American Civil Liberties Union 2004

The Supreme Court 5-4 upheld a judge's order that kept the government from enforcing the Child Online Protection Act of 1998. That Act would impose a $50,000 fine and six months in prison for the operator of a commercial website that posted "patently offensive" photos or descriptions that were available to minors. Website operators could defend themselves by requiring a credit card number or an adult access number to enter the site.

The justices stopped short of declaring the law unconstitutional. Instead they sent the case to a court in Philadelphia for a trial to decide whether software filters would work as well as a criminal law in shielding children from online pornography.

Consult your text and/or do an online search for:
U.S. v Extreme Assoc. **2005**
What did the material at issue deal with?

68 | Chapter 15 Obscenity and Pornography

What did the Supreme Court rule in this case?

What was the key element of the "Miller Test" that was a determining factor in the Court's ruling?

Study Guide Questions

Do a computer search to find the *Ashcroft v ACLU* case and summarize one of the minority opinions in the case.

Do an online search for the Time magazine, April 11, 2016 cover story for a recent article on the impact of sexually explicit material in society.

Do searches on the following and be able to explain or identify on an exam:
Anthony Comstock

Butler v Michigan 1957 (Laws cannot ban sexually explicit material from adults just because the material may be considered harmful to children.) Consider Section 343 of the Michigan Penal Code which makes it a misdemeanor to sell or make available to the general reading public any book containing obscene language "tending to the moral corruption of youth. What did Justice Frankfurter say in this case? (Mr. Butler sold the offending book to a police officer.)

Reno v ACLU **1997** (Internet is entitled to the highest First Amendment protection.)In 1997, a group of organizations, including the American Civil Liberties Union (ACLU), challenged the "indecent transmission" and "patently offensive display" provisions of the 1996 Communications Decency Act. These provisions made it a crime to send offensive Internet material to persons under age eighteen. The district court found for the ACLU. On behalf of the Federal Government, Attorney General Janet Reno appealed to the Supreme Court.

The Supreme Court invalidated both provisions of the Communications Decency Act (CDA) of 1996, because they violated the First Amendment's guarantee of freedom of speech. Justice John Paul Stevens wrote an opinion in which six other justices joined fully.

Justice Stevens reviewed the operation of the Internet and the difficulty of verifying the age of an Internet user. Justice Stevens pointed out several problems with the act: It did not define "indecent," it did not allow parents to authorize their children to access restricted materials, it applied "to the entire universe of cyberspace" rather than to well-defined areas. Moreover, the Internet is not a "scarce" commodity like the airwaves, so there is less justification for governmental regulation. Finally, the regulated materials do not just appear on the computer screen, but must be actively sought out.

Hannegan v. Esquire, Inc., **327 U.S. 146 (1946),** was a U.S. Supreme Court case argued between the United States Postal Service and *Esquire* magazine. In a unanimous decision, the Supreme Court ruled that the USPS was without statutory authority to revoke a periodical's second-class permit on the basis of objectionable material that was not obscene.

Jacobellis v Ohio **378 U.S. 184**
Appellant, manager of a motion picture theater, was convicted under a state obscenity law of possessing and exhibiting an allegedly obscene film, and the State Supreme Court upheld the conviction.

New York v. Ferber, **458 U.S. 747 (1982),** is a precedential decision given by the United States Supreme Court, which ruled unanimously that the First Amendment right to free speech did not forbid states from banning the sale of material depicting children engaged in sexual activity. SCOTUS on first examination of a statute specifically targeted against child pornography, it found that the state's interest in preventing sexual exploitation of minors was a compelling "government objective of surpassing importance." The law was carefully drawn to protect children from the mental, physical, and sexual abuse associated with pornography while not violating the First Amendment.

What are current efforts by the federal government to stop the spread of obscenity and pornography?

Go to 60Mins.com website and do a search for segments they have produced relating to the effects of pornography in our society. Summarize one in the space below.

Student Notes

Magazines

Chapter 16

The development of the magazine industry has played an important role in American history. Early magazines gave writers more time to do in-depth reporting and became a vital instrument of early muckrakers. Today magazines are a great example of segmentation of the media. Magazines are able to reach so many "niches" appealing to diverse reader values, needs, interests, beliefs, and attitudes.

List three magazines you view on a regular basis?

1.
2.
3.

What do these magazines offer that you cannot get through other media outlets?

Next time you are at an airport, note how much time you spend in the stores that display magazine titles.

Do you find yourself looking at magazines you have never noticed before? What are some of the new titles you are drawn to?

Do you find that if you buy a magazine at the airport, you are likely to read it more carefully than you do the ones you subscribe to at home? (You have to admit, being strapped in at 35,000 ft makes for a pretty "captive" audience.)

Chapter 16 Magazines

Study Guide Activities

Do Text and Online Search For:

Henry Luce

Time/Life Magazine

Modern trends in magazine production. Note the impact of the Internet on the magazine industry. Also note the move of magazine to online formats.

List three magazines you purchased off the stand in the last month.

Do you feel that "women's" magazines "cultivate" values like how women look and what they feel about their role in society? Explain.

Go to the magazine section at a local Barnes & Noble bookstore. List the magazines that appeal to young girls 10–13, then 14–18. List the advertisements most prominent in these publications.

1.
2.
3.
4.
5.
6.
7.
8.
9.

List four magazines that you feel would most appeal to men. Say why you think they may appeal to this demographic and list the advertisements most prominent in these publications.

What are "zines" and what is their role in society?

Go to the AdWeek website and search for the current list of their ranking of the year's "Hottest Magazine." What are their criteria for their ranking?

Student Notes

Chapter 17

The Muckrakers

The role of muckrakers in American media history has been a major factor in giving citizens here a quality of life that has been arguably the envy of the modern civilized world. Their efforts to investigate social ills or injustices in society were instrumental in initiating reforms. Throughout U.S. history, the media, empowered by the First Amendment to the U.S. Constitution, have used their guaranteed freedoms to give the public information they have both the need and the right to know.

During the academic term of this course, students are required to watch the *CBS News Magazine, 60 Minutes*. This requirement is not meant as an endorsement of the program as the "be all, end all" of television investigative programming. However, over the years, it has established a high level of credibility in the area of investigative news production. It is considered by many to be an example of modern-day muckraking. The program does generate important and many times controversial topics that make for excellent classroom discussion and debate. It is a good example of the "Power of the Fourth Estate."

It rarely beats popular programs like American Idol or Dancing with the Stars in the ratings but it many times does make the top 10 rated programs and thus shows "hope for our democracy."

Class Activity:

Form groups of two or three students. Together, research a selected or assigned "muckraker." (many are listed at the end of this study guide lesson)

Prepare a 3–5 min. PowerPoint to present to the class.
Be sure to include:

1. Name and pictures
2. What they investigated and what they found
3. What was the impact of their published investigation

Chapter 17 The Muckrakers

Study Guide Activities

Names and terms you will be required to know for exams. Use online searches, text, or library sources to elaborate on the contributions of the following:

Teddy Roosevelt: Where did the term "muckrakers" originate?

Horace Greely: *New York Tribune*. First to separate fact from opinion in the newspaper. Jacob Riis: An investigative journalist. Wrote *How the Other Half Lives*

Lincoln Steffens: *The Shame of the Cities*, a series of articles on how city government institutions work together to effect their own agendas.

Ray Stannard Baker: *McClure's* Magazine.

Charles Russell: Wrote about Georgia chain gangs' abuse, leading to prison reform.

Ida Tarbell: Investigated and wrote a 19-part series on the monopolistic excesses of Standard Oil and J.D. Rockefeller.

Upton Sinclair: Wrote *The Jungle*. Led to the Pure Food and Drug Act.

David Graham Phillips: Exposed corruption in the election of senators by state legislatures, leading to the Seventeenth Amendment to the U.S. Constitution.

Teapot Dome Scandal: President Harding and Secretary of the Interior Albert Fall.
Edward R. Morrow: McCarthyism.

Drew Pearson: The muckraker with a Quaker conscious.
Tad Schultz (also spelled Szulc): Bay of Pigs.

Daniel Ellsberg: *The Pentagon Papers*.

Carl Bernstein/Bob Woodward: *All the President's Men*—the Watergate Scandal.
We again mention here, the movie *Spotlight*. *This was a movie dealing with the Boston Globe's investigation into abuse by the Catholic Church.*

List some modern-day examples of journalistic "muckraking." (Think information related to government spending, war conduct, business scams, insider trading, political corruption including bribes, etc.) Note the number of bloggers engaging in investigative research regarding issues of public concern.

Student Notes

Persuasive Media: Advertising

Chapter 18

Use text, library, and online sources to familiarize yourself with the historical background regarding advertising.

Advertisers use words and images to persuade us to take some action. Most often the purpose of commercial advertising is to get us to part with some of our hard-earned money. Political ads use words and images to persuade us to vote for a certain issue or candidate.

Through your educational journey, instructors have put a premium on thinking logically. Logical thinking is the kind of thinking we do when we consider the results of certain actions. Logical thinking is based on evidence. Logical thinking requires putting words together in statements and putting statements together to arrive at conclusions.

It is important to realize that we all occasionally engage in other forms of mental activity, including daydreaming, reminiscing, and making random associations. Students, however, must make important distinctions between the benefits of these forms of thinking and logical thinking.

Some common blocks to our logical thinking process take into account our respective beliefs, values, needs, and attitudes. Some of these become a preconceived prejudice or ready-made judgments. Many times strong emotions, influenced by values and beliefs, can block our logical thinking process.

Again, one of the great things about this course is that we can find current media examples for this exercise to discuss in class. Here are some common fallacies of logical thinking that people in the persuasive media business use to influence us.

1. **Hasty Conclusions** (Secundum Quid): This fallacy occurs when a generalization is made before enough specific items have been examined. Keys to this fallacy come when we hear the word "**ALL**" or the words and images used infer that all the items should be included.

   Examples:

2. **Appealing to Authority** (Ad Verecundiam): It is natural that we develop a certain level of respect for parents, teachers, clergy, doctors, and other professionals. We also associate a level of authority with items presented as statistics, charts, and more.

   However, when these symbols are used out of context or are presented in a way where the authority is not named or verified, we should be careful. Another aspect of this fallacy is the appeal to potential incompetent authorities. This fallacy is sometimes referred to as the "big name" fallacy. We need to make sure that the person being used as an authority on a product or issue really does know a lot about the subject.

Examples:

3. **Appeal to the Crowd** (Ad Populum): This is one of the most popular of the advertising/propaganda techniques. There are three parts to this fallacy:

   a. Flag waving: This fallacy appeals to our love of America and American institutions and symbols to get us to take an action or buy a product we might not otherwise consider.

   Examples:

   b. Bandwagon: Most of us want to feel we belong. This fallacy either says or shows "everybody" getting behind the issue or product and "you do not want to be left behind."

   Examples:

   c. Reverse bandwagon: Here we pick up the people who "are not like everyone else." They are the independent operators who do not like being like everyone else. So they become part of a group of millions to whom advertisers appeal with certain ads.

   Examples:

   d. Tear jerking: It is important to be caring and even sympathetic to causes or issues. But let's be logical in evaluating how much of our contributions really go to the cause being promoted and how much goes to "administration." Commercial-product advertisers use this fallacy as well.

   Examples:

4. **False Analogies:** Analogies are comparisons. We use comparisons often to help make a point. Advertisers, politicians (and, yes, your college instructors) know this, so we need to check to make sure that the things being compared have enough points in common.

   Examples:

5. **Faulty Dilemmas:** This fallacy occurs when only two choices are given when more actually exist. Key words in this fallacy are "either/or."

   Examples:

6. **The Hidden Major Premise:** This fallacy relies on our acquired knowledge about inductive and deductive logic. The classic form of deductive logic is a syllogism. A syllogism has three main parts. First is the major premise, which usually begins with the word "all." It is followed by the minor premise which is linked to the major premise but is more detailed. Finally is the conclusion. A = B, B = C. Therefore: A = C.

   All mammals are warm blooded. Whales are warm blooded. Therefore: Whales are mammals.

   In first grade, the teacher holds up a picture and asks us what we can learn from looking at this picture or what can we deduce from the picture? The fallacy occurs when advertisers, with words and images, lead you to a conclusion that has not been supported by a major premise. They purposely fail to STATE the premise upon which the conclusion is based.

   Lots of examples:

7. **Meaningless Words:** Words have both denotative and connotative meanings. Advertisers can use words is such a way and with special emphasis so that the words seem to have special meaning when they do not.

   Examples: Smoother, mellower, better tasting. It "conditions" your skin, "Come up to the Kool taste", etc.

   Other examples:

8. **You Too** (Tu Quoque): This fallacy occurs when we rotate a charge upon one's accuser. Two negatives only add up to a positive in math, not in our social or political life. Two wrongs do not make a right. This fallacy is often found in political advertising.

   Examples:

9. **After This Because of This** (Post Hoc, Ergo Propter Hoc): We will not be using this fallacy to evaluate advertising. However, this argument is often tried in political debate. It is an error in the understanding of the cause and effect relationship. It is assumed that just because an event follows another in time, the first is the cause of the second.

   Examples:

82 | Chapter 18   Persuasive Media: Advertising

10. **Begging or Ignoring the Question** (Argumentum Ignorare): A question is posed in an ad but never directly answered. A public figure or official is asked an important question but spends time talking about everything but the answer to the question.
    Examples:

11. **Getting Personal** (Ad Hominem): Many times in political debate, candidates will stop addressing the issues and start attacking the personal life of their opponent. This fallacy is also many times referred to as "name calling" or "mudslinging."
    Examples:

Other Terms and Issues Covered on Exams

Advertising agencies

Consumer advertising

Creative boutiques

Marketing

Federal Trade Commission

First advertisements in colonial America

Evidence of advertising in Roman society

Ad copy

Caveat emptor

Current trends in coordinating television "advertising pods"

Current trends to make television ads more entertaining (List at least three examples from current television advertising.)

Abraham Maslow's Hierarchy of Needs (from the bottom)

1. Physiological: hunger and thirst.
2. Safety: law and order (security from danger).
3. Belongingness and Love: to be accepted.
4. Esteem: to achieve; to be competent.
5. Cognitive: to know; to explore.
6. Aesthetic: order and beauty in the universe.
7. Self-actualization: realize your own potential; be self-fulfilled.

How do advertisers play to these "needs" to add value to their respective products? Give three examples of advertisements on television that play specifically to one or more of Maslow's list of human needs.

Tear three ads out of a magazine and identify which level of Maslow's Hierarchy of Needs the ad appeals to.

The course/study guide blog has flash card elements for this lesson as well as Quizlet questions. (Go to reedsmassmedia.wordpress.com)

Student Notes

Tear three ads out of a magazine that you think are really well done. Then, after analyzing them in light of the "common fallacies", list the fallacies you think the advertiser may be using in each respective ad.

Persuasive Media: Propaganda

Chapter 19

The world of words includes connotations and denotations. Words can be used in different ways with different effects. Propaganda takes advantage of this fact. As you have learned in the "logical thinking" unit on advertising, words used in certain contexts illicit very emotional responses. Here we again see how words and images are used to persuade individuals and/or groups to take a course of action they might not ordinarily take.

The book/video *Faces of the Enemy* by Sam Keen, a noted author, social observer and commentator, gives some examples of how words and images are used to effect an end. The dictionary definitions for the word **propaganda** are:

1. Publicity to promote something: information or publicity put out by an organization or government to spread and promote an idea, doctrine, or cause.
2. Misleading publicity: deceptive or distorted information that is systematically spread. However, there are many feelings and emotions tied to the word as well.

Generally propaganda is associated with the use of highly charged images and words to move to action. The most important lesson learned is, Keen says, that before we are moved to war, we have to CREATE an image of the enemy. He gives us several poignant examples including an example related to a 1945 U.S. propaganda film about the Japanese and another example from a 1938 Nazi film about Jews.

Study Guide Activities

Do an online search for Sam Keen, *Faces of the Enemy* (book and film).

What insights does Keen make into "enemy making"?

What analogies were drawn in the referenced WWII Nazi propaganda films?

Chapter 19 Persuasive Media: Propaganda

What did American WWII propaganda films propose Americans do?

According to Keen, before we go to war we have to create _____.

What are some of the propaganda techniques you have studied in this class that are used by America to goad citizens to actions they might not otherwise take?
Keen wants us to consider:

In the end it is easier not to talk, think, and feel. If we view our enemies as abstractions, that makes what easier?

What is the role of cartoonists?

Whose side is God on?

We are good, they are evil.
We are honest, they are liars.
We are heroes, they are villains.
Individual action versus national action

In election years, use "fact checking" sources to hold political figures accountable for their respective statements in debates and in ads.

Film

Chapter 20

The impact of motion pictures on society is well documented. The digital age has marked another revolutionary era in film history. Hollywood has had a major impact on the basic values, needs, beliefs, attitudes, and more of Americans. Many felt with the advent of the video cassette and DVDs, movie theaters would go out of business. Instead they have proliferated. In fact, these new technological advances, including MP3 players, Netflix downloading of movies directly into homes, and more have enhanced the revenue of the big movie houses.

Kinetoscope

- 24: In 1878, Edward Muybridge placed 24 cameras next to each other at a race track; what resulted was static images that create a motion effect
    - Ever heard of 24 frames per second?
- Edison: Thomas Edison and William Dickson developed the first motion camera
- Kinetoscope: In 1889, Dickson place holes in the side of the reel to create quick succession
- Vitascope: Edison perfected projector arrives in 1896

The Early Days

- Nickelodeons (or nickelettes): These pre-movie theatre venues seated 50 to 90 people and cost 5 cents for admission. Since films were were short in length they turned over content daily.
- Adapting Theatre: Prior to a more fully-realized film language (film editing, cinematography, set design, etc.) filmmakers like Adolph Zukor filmed plays and played their recordings on big screens.
- *Birth of a Nation*: Without a script, Griffith created a civil war epic (complete with some of the most racist blackface ever), employing film techniques in a whole new way
    - Censorship: Many complaints arose regarding the film's racist undertones, but since all censorship boards were white little to nothing was done
- Block Booking: To receive top films from a studio, theatres had to agree to play twice as many other films from the studio

The Motion Picture Patents Company (MPPC)

- Equipment: Royalty-free bootleg equipment emerged, so the Big 9 studios used a $2 weekly tax to thwart competition, resulting in police raids and destroyed equipment
- Go West: In response, indie filmmakers migrated from the East to West Coast, settling in the Los Angeles area because of its close proximity to diverse landscape.

The Star System

- Celebrity Culture: In L.A., studios began to promote stars rather than studios, which lead to the formation of United Artists, thanks to stars like Mary Pickford and Charlie Chaplin.
- Length: Actors wanted more screen time, so films got longer, one to two hours.
- Theatres: Formal viewing locations, theatres, eventually began to develop, including more comfortable seating
- Costs: Ticket prices increased along with theatre development and film production.

The Studio System

Control of all three: Production, distribution, and exhibition

- Production: Creation of the film itself—all costs involved.
- Distribution: Negotiate take for tickets, ensure enough reels are available for opening day, and market the film with posters, trailers, and other ads; as for home video, deals regarding DVDs and Blu-Rays (a Sony company).
- Exhibition: The theatre itself which determines showtimes, number of screenings, etc.; it can even determine trailer counts.

Anti-Trust Laws & the Big Screen

- Share the Wealth: In 1938, the Justice Department criticized film studios, claiming they had a monopoly on the film industry by controlling production, distribution, and exhibition.
- No Trust: In United States v Paramount Pictures, Inc. 1948, the Supreme Court rules film studios cannot own distribution and exhibition of films.
- The Big 8: Eight studio systems were affected influenced by this ruling, including Columbia Pictures, Fox Film Corporation, Loew's Incorporated (part of Metro-Goldwyn-Mayer), Paramount Pictures, RKO Radio Pictures, United Artists, Universal Pictures, and Warner Bros.

The Aftermath

- Block booking went away
- Golden Age: Thus ended the Golden Age of Cinema as studios began to cut back on production (1927–1949).
- TV: The expansion of television also cut into film audiences, particularly ending film serials.
- Gimmicks: Film studios would eventually advertise changing technologies – wider screens, 3D, technicolor – to bring audiences back.

The Blockbuster

- Fragmentation: When film lost its universal appeal, box office revenue decreased.
- New Hollywood: Starting in the late 1960s, this era changed the tone of films; they ended up either darker (*The Godfather*, *Taxi Driver*) or faster paced (*Jaws*, *Star Wars*).
- Movie Brats: The first generation of filmmakers to go through film school: Steven Spielberg, George Lucas, Martin Scorsese, Francis Ford Coppola, Robert Altman, Stanley Kubrick, and Paul Schrader.

Evolving Trends

- ID: Independent producers provided competition for major studios.
- Made for TV: Suddenly, studios began making films specifically for television.
- Less Films: The number of theatrical releases decreased (something that continues to occur with major studio hoping for more blockbuster films and less passion projects).
- A Few Wins: Now the structure is a few big films to pay for all the failures (or quid pro co for actors).

Later Changes

- VCR: Now, households could wait until something was out on video—no longer just theatres.
- DVD/Blu-ray: Digital copies that lasted longer, less erosion, quicker to navigate, extras.
- Streaming: More options than we can ever fathom.
- Classic Model: The majority of profit is still DVD sales (Blu-ray helped a bit), but consumers prefer digital copies and streaming.

The Digital Era

- Digital Conversion: Classic film vs. digital formats.
- All Digital: CGI and blue/green technology.
- Distribution: Films reels are still shipped to most theatres, but some films are digitally sent (new problems with getting hacked or intercepted).
- Digital Projection: No longer do we have those pesky dots appearing all over the screen.
- 3D: Some are created with it in mind or post-converted; either way, 3D greatly increases a film's profits through the simple sale of glasses.

The Digital Home

- On Demand: After Blockbuster and Hollywood Video died, Apple TV, Xbox 360/One, Playstation 3/4, Roku, Chromecast, etc. took over; and let's not forget about Redbox.
- Mobile Devices: Films get smaller and go where you go, not just planes anymore.
- User-Generated Filmmaking: This is more a dream at the moment, but we might eventually see studios incorporate more content from users, like the Star Wars film festival.
- Social Media: Promotion has entirely changed thanks to this.

Cinema's Big 6 Today

- Sony/MGM
- NBC Universal
- Disney
- Fox
- Warner Bros.
- Paramount

Feedback

- Box office revenue
- DVD sales
- Streaming data
- Reviews/aggregation websites like Rotten Tomatoes
- Nielson ratings

Did You Know . . .

- January is where movies go to die since it's the lowest movie-going month of the year.
- If you hear nothing about a film prior to its release, it didn't test well with pre-screenings, so the studio decided to place a media blackout on it until the day before the film's premiere.
- Once a film premieres, its box office profits cut in half every weekend; good films drop 40%, bad ones drop 60%.

The Production Process

Preproduction

- Treatment: Plot description, some dialogue, characters
- Script: First draft, revised, script polish
- Funding: Where's the money coming from? Studios or independent production (*Cloud Atlas* is the most expensive independently-funded film of all time)
- Talent: Locate stars, producers, directors, etc.

Production

- Day to Day: Average cost for a day is $400,000 to $500,000
- Shooting: Average 70 days of shooting, resulting in 2 minutes of usable footage per day

Postproduction

- Special Effects: Added elements afterwards, like filling in green screens
- Editing: Choosing which shots best suit a scene, adding music, etc.

Citizen Kane Study Guide Released 1941, RKO

Orson Welles, starred, directed, supervised casting, and coauthored the script.

He made his mark in media production with the 1938 War of the Worlds radio broadcast. Welles was 25 years old when he made Citizen Kane.

It took Welles six months to film and less $1 million to produce the film.

- Number One on the American Film Institute's list of the 100 Greatest Movies
- Number Four on the Writers Guild of America list of the 101 greatest screenplays ever. (After *Casablanca*, *The Godfather*, and *Chinatown*.)

Plot: Life of Charles Foster Kane (parody on William Randolph Hearst)

Lecture: Research and discuss the parallels of the movie character and the real media mogul.

Sound: echo, recorded sound effects, and music to tell the story: Specific examples from the film:

Technique: newsreel, camera angles, flashback, zoom, lighting techniques, and use of light to set the mood for the telling of the story, also use of light and shadow to show power.

Use of the hook: Rosebud

Specific examples from the film:

Aging of the actors—use of makeup. Find scenes where the use of short vignettes to explain a relationship and move the story. (hints: marriage, scene near the end when characters speak in a large room with fireplace)

List some of the parallels you find in your online research between the fictional Kane character and William Randolph Hearst.

Outline here information from the course blog on Citizen Kane.
Look under: Film heading

Study Guide Activities

Through online searches, text, and other information resources identify the following:

Hays Production Code

Chapter 20 Film

Birth of a Nation

Charlie Chaplin

"Star system"

Motion picture rating systems

Books to read when you have time:
<u>The Chief</u> by David Nasaw
<u>Citizen Hearst</u> by W. A. Swanberg

Study Guide Questions

Possible Exam Essay Question:
Rent the CD of *Citizen Kane*: Write a short essay explaining why the American Film Institute ranks the film the best film of all time.

Based on box office ratings at the time you are taking the course, what does the American public seem to value most on the "big screen"?

Chapter 21
Public Relations

Public relations (PR) practitioners seek free time and space in the media. Advertising is purchased time and space in the media. Through class lecture and PowerPoint presentation, the following public relations factors will be presented and discussed.

Some skills to consider in Public Relations campaigns:

1. Learn to write a press release in the Associated Press style.
2. Network: join local and regional press clubs, local chambers of commerce, and service organizations. Contact gatekeepers and ask them to lunch.
3. Be opportunistic: Look for ways to set your business apart from the rest. Learn to read the small print and take advantage of special circumstances. Learn and study the content of the many special sections and departments of electronic media.
4. Learn to take pictures: Take classes that teach you how to take photos that look good in print. Learn the different capabilities of digital cameras and the computer software associated with them.
5. Always think and plan ahead.
6. Learn how to organize and host a press day or special event.
7. Learn how to develop and deliver a PowerPoint presentation: Know that a picture is worth a thousand words. Images should be displayed not less than three seconds and not more than five.
8. High tech/high touch: Learn to be personable. Know the importance of hand-written thank you notes.
9. Study local media deadlines. Know the four elements of news: impact, timeliness, proximity, and credibility.
10. Make sure to be honest and straightforward.
11. Learn to be a good public speaker.
12. Develop and/or subscribe to media contact data banks.

Chapter 21 Public Relations

Most historians agree that the first real public relations pioneer was Ivy Lee. In 1903, Lee and George Parker opened a publicity office. During the Pennsylvania coal operators strike, Lee issued a "Declaration of Principles," which included "be open and honest." After WWI, Carl Byoir and Edward L. Bernays came on the scene. Bernays wrote the first book on public relations, _Crystallizing Public Opinion_, published in 1923.

Study Guide Activities

Please do an online search to find out more about Ivy Lee and Edward L. Bernays.
List important elements of what you find:

Through text, online, and other sources define or identify:
Spin doctors

PR tactical plans

Management-by-objective PR (MBO)

Integrated marketing communications (IMC)

Areas with public relations interests: (Explain the function of each.)
1. Business

2. Government and politics

3. Educational institutions (Including sports departments)

4. Hospitals

5. Nonprofits

6. Professional organizations (attorneys, doctors, dentists, etc)

7. The entertainment industry

8. Professional sports

9. Environmental organizations

Explain the "crisis management" function of public relations. Give an example

Explain the impact of social media on public relations. Give examples.

Create a list of public relations jobs in your geographic region.

Student Notes

Impact of New Media

Chapter 22

The impact of online delivery systems is having an immense impact on how we interact with family, friends, school, work, businesses, government, and more. Cell phones make communication faster and more mobile. The Internet makes almost all aspect of life more expedient. We are able to research movies, restaurants, doctors, lawyers, teachers, health issues, and just about every aspect of our day-to-day wants and needs. The ability to access emergency help and report crime even to the point of being able to record such with cellphone cameras, has become an important factor in everyday life. This mass communication phenomenon fueled by daily technological innovations and development can have a down side. Invasion of privacy issues, car accident impacts, human predator issues, accessibility of sexually explicit material concerns, not to mention intergovernmental "hacking" and monitoring of terrorist networks, are all being addressed by academic institutions, government security officers, and elected officials nationwide. It is incumbent upon college students to be well versed in the basics of social media and to engage in vigorous debate regarding its positive and negative impacts.

Impact:

- **Wiki's** (i.e. Wikimedia, Wikipedia, WikiCommons, WikiLeaks): Wiki means quick in Hawaiian. Wikipedia is one of the most popular resources on the Web. It is an "open editing" model which allows anyone to edit and contribute to articles. This type of forum often gets criticized as a reliable source of information.

    Study Question: Why is Wikipedia not a stand-alone reliable source for obtaining information?

- **Blogs:** Internet Web logs. These are user created sites that contain posts/articles that allow interaction with readers such as comments or links to other articles posted on the Web.
    1. In 2006, more than 12 million adults created blogs.
    2. In 2006, 39% of Internet users read blogs.
    3. As of March 17, 2011, 73% of Internet users went online to get information about the 2010 mid-term election as sited from the Pew Internet & American Life Project study.

- **Mobile devices:** smart phones, iPads, tablet computers.
    1. As of March 2011, 47% of U.S. adults got some form of news on their phone or tablet computer.
    2. Of that 47%, only 1 in 10 use an app to get their information instead of a browser.
- Lists some of the present impacts of the WikiLeaks site.

Sociological Impacts:

- **Internet groups** (i.e. Facebook, Instagram): 80% of all users participate in some form of online group. Instagram is an online mobile photo-sharing, video-sharing, and social networking service that enables its users to take pictures and videos, and share them either publicly or privately on the app, as well as through a variety of other social networking platforms, such as Facebook, Twitter, Tumblr, and Flickr.
    1. These groups include Facebook groups of organizations
- By 2010, most people had shifted to social networking instead of blogging
    1. History of MySpace and its impact on the Millennial Generation:
        a. Founded in 2003 and by 2007 boasted 188 million individual profiles
        b. It served as a place for people to put updates, pictures and music, the last allowing users to buy songs from the site
        c. In 2006, the site goes international, opening servers in the UK, Japan and France, and finally China in 2007
        d. Paved the way for the social networking giant Facebook
    2. Problems/consequences:
        a. Concerns by schools, parents and law enforcement that the publicity of social networking sites is an invitation to predators
        b. Real world example: (a girl was denied her degree because of photos on her Myspace)
    3. Some interesting updated stats from 2015:
    4. 2.4 billion people around the world use the Internet (out of 7 billion).
    5. 8.7 billion machines are connected to the Internet (including smartphones, tablets, refrigerators, soda pop machines . . .
    6. 78% of North Americans use the Internet.
    7. Facebook has 1.4 billion users worldwide.

    Sites such as Craigslist allow users to post items they are selling, real estate listings, and any other product they wish to share in an open forum

Political Impacts:

- April 2011: President Obama announces his re-election via an online video.
- April 11, 2011, former Massachusetts Governor Mitt Romney announced his Republican presidential bid through online video.
- After breaking off budget talks with Republican, California Governor Jerry Brown took his case to voters through a video posted on YouTube.
- Other political members have used Twitter, Facebook, and other social media not only to inform voters but also to slam their opponents as opposed to simply relying on commercials during elections.
- Candidates can directly reach voters platforms where they work and play—YouTube, Facebook, and Twitter
- In 2012, Republicans Tim Pawlenty and Mitt Romney announced their respective presidential aspirations via Facebook and Twitter.

2016 Candidate Donald Trump uses Twitter to attack other candidates.

Study Questions

What has been the impact of Craigslist on newspapers?

Do an online search for the debate on "net neutrality" the principle that individuals should be free to access all content and applications equally, regardless of the source, without Internet service providers discriminating against specific online services or websites.
Supporters say. . . . ?
Opponents say. . . . ?
The FCC voted on February 26, 2015 that it could make net neutrality rules based on the powers given them in the 1934 Federal Communications Act

What is the impact of Twitter and Facebook on restaurants, retail, travel, and other businesses?

Write a short page and a half essay, typed double-spaced on how you would use "new media" to enhance a business you might start or work for.

Chapter 22 Impact of New Media

What is the impact on society of text messaging? Remind, WeChat, Facebook Messenger, SnapChat, WhatsApp, Skype and others. Note the unique features of each.

What about the impact of new steaming television?
List the unique features of:

Apple TV

Amazon Fire TV

Google Chromecast

Roku 4

More than 100 internet video streaming service are available. A few of the more popular:

Amazon Prime

CBS All Access

Crackle

Crunchyroll

Dove Channel

DramaFeaver

HBO Now

Hulu

LucasOilRacing.TV

MLB.TV

Netflix

NFL Game Pass

Noggin

SeeSo

Sling TV

Showtime

Smithsonian Earth

Tennis Channel Plus

TheBlaze TV

Univision Now

WWE Network

YouTube Red

Note the service you use. List the cost (if any) and the unique feature that led you to subscribe.

It is appropriate to note here Facebook's work on developing its "virtual-reality" device Oculus. What is the status of this development at the time you are studying New Media?

It is also instructive to note the auto industries led by Tesla and Google toward self-driving cars. At the time you are taking this course, what is the status of this development?

This Movie is recommended: View the movie and turn in a 2-page, typed double spaced review.

The Social Network is a 2010 American biographical drama film directed by David Fincher and written by Aaron Sorkin. Adapted from Ben Mezrich's 2009 book *The Accidental Billionaires: The Founding of Facebook, A Tale of Sex, Money, Genius, and Betrayal*, the film portrays the founding of social networking website Facebook and the resulting lawsuits. It stars Jesse Eisenberg as founder Mark Zuckerberg, along with Andrew Garfield as Eduardo Saverin and Justin Timberlake as Sean Parker, the other principals involved in the website's creation. Neither Zuckerberg nor any other Facebook staff were involved with the project, although Saverin was a consultant for Mezrich's book. The film was released in the United States by Columbia Pictures on October 1, 2010.

Students may want to read the book **Steve Jobs by Walter Isaacson** and/or do an online search for Steve Jobs and write and two page paper on how he impacted "new media"

Student Notes

List of Resources

The Structure and Function of Communication in Society in the Communication of Ideas (New York, Harper, 1948)

Milestones in Mass Communication Theories and Research: Media Effects (New York, Longman, 1983)

Introduction to Mass Communication by Black, Bryant (McGraw Hill, 1998)

Miracle at Philadelphia by Catherine Drinker Bowen

Major Principles of Media Law by Overbeck (1990)

http://www.socialhistory.org/biographies by Harrison Gray Otis, Harry Chandler, Norman Chandler

Californians and the Military, Major-General Harrison Gray Otis by Mark Denger, found at www.militarymuseum.org/Otis

Los Angeles Times, October 1, 1919, Front Page *The Powers That Be* by David Halberstam *Harrison Gray Otis* by Albert Greenstein

Otis Chandler 1927–2006, "A Lion of Journalism." *L.A. Times*, February 28, 2006, Special Section

"Aubrey: A Lion in Winter," *L.A. Times*, April 27, 1986, Calendar Section

Newsweek, November 8, 2010

Appendices

Journalism Program Goal Statement **106**

Course Research Paper **108**

Term Project Course Requirements **110**

Student Special Project: Native Americans in the Media **113**

Please note: Power Point and/or Prezi presentations are available for each lesson. Contact the Journalism Department, Saddleback College, Mission Viejo CA, 92692.

Journalism Program Goal Statement

Many journalism programs recognize the significance of the 2005 Carnegie Corporation of New York report "Improving the Education of Tomorrow's Journalists." This report was the culmination of research and interviews with the nation's most prominent publishers, presidents, chairmen, editors, anchors, senior correspondents, and producers about the state of journalism education and what journalism schools might do to elevate the profession's standards and status.

These findings and recommendations correspond with research, interviews, and evaluation conducted by various local, regional, and state program administrative and instructional staff through sabbatical leave research and study, alumni survey, and correspondence, student survey, and test results. These findings are reflected in the educational goals of many respected college/high school journalism programs.

1. The journalism program recognizes and promotes the fact that it is understood in our country that journalism is central to the strength and vitality of American democracy. The press, an institution outside government, was included among the civic organizations and activities to be protected by the Bill of Rights. A free press, the founders believed, was essential to keeping watch on the affairs of government and creating an active, politically informed public. (Carnegie Report p.1)

2. The journalism program emphasizes the basics of the journalism craft along with analytical thinking and a strong sense of ethics. This includes the basic writing skills, as well as the paramount importance of getting the facts right. Students need to develop good news judgment and analytical skills, including the ability to separate fact from opinion and use statistics correctly. (Carnegie Report p.3 and 6)

3. The journalism program helps student reporters understand the importance of developing specialized expertise to enhance their coverage of complex beats, from medicine to economics, and help students acquire first-hand knowledge of the societies, languages, religions, and cultures of other parts of the world.

4. The journalism program seeks to identify and channel the best writers, the most curious reporters, and the most analytical thinkers into the profession of journalism.

Others findings of the Carnegie Corporation Report that are recognized and discussed across the journalism curriculum include:

1. Concern about the media's quest for profits and audience. The report concludes the most critical responsibility of journalists is to serve the public interest and protect our democracy.

2. The challenge for journalism and journalists is to find ways to interest readers and viewers in news that is vital to a functioning democracy.

3. The concern that much of the news has too much "edge," particularly from "talking head" shows on cable news and radio.

4. Concern that a shorter-attention span among the public forces reporters to make the news fast and exciting. This leads to concern about training prospective reporters to know even more about complex beats if they are to deliver stories that are both shorter and more interesting.

5. The report also expressed a concern that young students aspire to become on-air television reporters and anchors without first mastering the skills of hard news reporting.
6. The report could not overemphasize the importance of upholding the ethics of journalism. They believe that the ethical ramifications of journalism must be infused throughout the curriculum, not just taught in ethics classes.
7. The report mentions the importance of working on the college newspaper as an excellent preparation for a journalism career.

Course Research Paper

Students transferring to a four-year college or university must exhibit a proficiency in writing a research paper using proper documentation. In this course, students will be required to turn in a 3–5 page mini-research paper.

Students may select other media-related topics but only upon instructor approval. Students must cite from at least three different sources in the text of their mini-paper.

The accepted method of documentation for this paper will be the Modern Language Association (MLA) method. MLA uses parenthetical references within the text keyed to a Works Cited list at the end of the mini-paper.

A typical reference would include the author's name and a page number. If you use the author's name and the title of the work cited in the text, then the page number is all that is required at the end of the paragraph. Please check your English course text for more examples.

The college's Learning Assistance Program (LAP) also provides resources for review of this method of documentation. The college library also provides a 2–3 page handout outlining the proper MLA format. It is pretty much expected that, upon high school graduation, students have been introduced to this or some other universally accepted method for attributing information in a research paper. To quote or paraphrase information from another source without giving credit can lead to charges of plagiarism.

Many students turn to the Internet for research. Please remember that information and articles must be properly cited in the text and on the works cited page. These citations most often include authors' names and pages cited or brief article titles and page number if the article is not authored.

Works Cited pages should include only works cited. If other sources were used and you would like to include them, please label the reference page a "Works Consulted" page.

Remember, even Supreme Court opinions are authored and, of course, opinions on the opinions are authored.

Note: Examples offered by course instructor in class.

Mini Papers Topics

1. The impact of Internet gambling on society.
2. The impact of on-line pornography on society.
3. The impact of cell phones on society.
4. Career options for journalism and communications majors.
5. The polarization of American: radio and television news.
6. Polarization of America: radio talk shows.
7. The impact of the internet on newspaper circulation. The future of newspapers in America.
8. The impact of the Internet on magazines. The future of magazines in America.
9. The impact of cell phones on the motion picture industry.
10. The impact of the Internet on the music industry.

11. The impact of the Internet on the motion picture industry.
12. The level of basic knowledge of and understanding of the U.S. Constitution by students in the eighth grade locally.
13. How important is the First Amendment to the U.S. Constitution to high schools students locally? Nationally? How many know the four freedoms listed in the First Amendment? How important is "the public's right to know?"
14. How important is the First Amendment to parents locally? (Minimum of 50 surveys.)
15. What is the impact of social media on society?

Students must use primary research methods. (Surveys: at least 50) Survey questions must be presented to the professor prior to distribution. In the 3–5 page paper, relate the findings of your primary research and link it to research on the topic you do on the Internet. Use at least two Internet sources. Provide a thesis statement and a conclusion that sums up your findings.

Term Project Course Requirements

An Introduction

Former students email the journalism program chair from their status as upper-division students at four-year colleges and universities stating that the term project they completed for their Mass Media and Society class was one of the most important assignments they completed, not just in the course, but some add that it proved to be one of the most important assignments completed while an undergraduate student. Some students are able to go back to the institution or business where they conducted their interview for the project and obtain an internship to fulfill their upper-division requirement in that area. Many students conduct an interview in an area in which they are interested only to find out, after the interview project, that this is NOT an area of communications they would like to pursue.

It is suggested that you select a media job you think you might like to have one day. It is important that you begin the process of scheduling your interview within the first few weeks of class. People working in the media, as with most professions, are very busy and need plenty of lead-time to set time aside for an interview. Students are encouraged to move outside their own circle of friends and relatives for interview possibilities. All students MUST clear their term project subject with the course instructor **prior** to the interview.

Term Project Guidelines

Project grade weight to be determined by instructors

First: Call a local or regional media source and tell them you are enrolled in a Mass Media and Society course and you need to interview someone at a media-related business for a class term project worth one quarter of your semester grade.

It helps to have a tape recorder or other recording device. It also helps to have a camera because you are **required** to have a picture of you with the person you interview, at the place where they are employed, included on the cover/title page of your report.

What area of media you are most interested in; public relations, print journalism, advertising, T.V., radio, etc? Try to pick a person with a broad background in the area of your choice. Pick someone who can answer most of the provided questions. If the media personality you chose cannot answer all the questions, maybe they can direct you to someone at the business who can. It is possible to interview someone outside your local community or region with the instructor's permission.

Next: Go IN PERSON and conduct an interview at the person's place of business. The interview MUST be in person and not over the phone. Get a picture of you with the person, with you, at the person's place of work. NO HOME BUSINESSES! Person interviewed must be a full-time employee.

Make sure to take a recording device to record the interview but also take written notes in case something goes wrong with the recording. Be sure to get permission to record from the person you interview before beginning the formal interview.

1. Background and history of the publication or business.
2. Publication circulation, estimated audience, or number of clients.
3. The geographic area served by the business.
4. How many editions, programs, or services are associated with this business or publication?
5. What are the demographics and psychographics of the audience served?
6. What are the gatekeeping policies of this media source? Who makes the editorial decisions? Who are the gatekeepers?
7. What or who provide the main competition?
8. Where do the revenues come from to support this media business?
9. If they have advertising, how much does it cost and to whom do they sell? Does the business accept community feedback?
10. What jobs are available in this business? What is the best entry-level position? What are the wages one could expect for various job descriptions within this media business? (Be sure to ask for salary ranges, do not ask for the specific salary of the person you are interviewing) Is the position paid hourly, salaried, do they pay stringers or freelancers?
11. Does the business sponsor internships?
12. How does the person you are interviewing like his or her job? What are their specific duties and responsibilities? What are the positive and negative aspects of their job?
13. What educational and/or vocational training is necessary for most full-time positions at this business? What are the best places to get this education or training?
14. What are the job benefits? (Insurance, perks, freebies, payola, junkets, other) These questions serve as a guideline. You are expected to develop your own questions both before and during the interview. Not all the questions apply to all businesses so improvise and come up with some of your own questions.
15. What is the "online" presence of the business? What do they feel is the impact of online delivery systems?
16. What is the future of print journalism?
17. What is the impact of social media?
18. Try to relate some of your class lecture, terms, and issues you have discussed in class. Ask them questions about how pertinent the information you have learned is to the real world of mass communication.

Be sure to include your evaluation of the assignment at the end of your interview.
No Q and A formats. Write the report as a personal essay or feature story. The reports should be typed double spaced, 8–10 pages long.

Cover page:

Term Project
Journalism 1, Mass Media and Society
Professor J. Mike Reed

Your Name
Date
Time your class meets

(Put the picture in this space!!)

Name of the business you visited
Address of business
Phone number of business
(Number you used to make your contact for interview)
Name and title of the person you interviewed

Please staple the cover page to your report for presentation to the professor. It is preferred you do not use cover folders.

5 extra credit points may be awarded for reports handed in the week before due date.

Projects handed in late may have points deducted at the instructor's discretion.

No projects accepted after last regular class meeting.

Student Special Project: Native Americans in the Media

Voices and Dreams

Native American History, Literature, Art, and Culture

Project created as part of a 1997
National Endowment for the Humanities
Seminar

Student Special Project: Native Americans in the Media

Stated objectives in the course outline for JRN/CA 1, Mass Media and Society reveal that students will engage the topic of ethnic minorities in the media. The course deals not only with treatment of women and racial minorities but it also explores the effects of under representing and misrepresenting women and minorities in the media.

The summer 1997 "Voices and Dreams" seminar at Saddleback College presented several valuable resources for exploring the treatment of Native Americans in the Media.

Students will use these resources to fulfill the mini-paper or special survey requirements for the media course.

To fulfill the "Treatment of the Native American" in the media requirement, the student will read, discuss, and answer short essay questions relating to the content of the four listed chapters in the book *Shadows of the Indian* by Raymond William Stedman.

Chapter 4, Indian Talk
- Lone Ranger radio broadcasts and telecasts
- TV Yancy Derringer series
- Last of the Mohicans
- Nick of the Woods

Chapter 8, The Enemy
In novel and film, virtually all surprise attacks on peaceful travelers from concealed position were the work of Indians.

Chapter 13, Mea Culp
- Stagecoach
- The Way West
- Cheyenne Autumn
- Soldier Blue
- A Man Called Horse
- Fort Apache
- Little Big Man
- I Will Fight No More Forever

Chapter 14, Lingering Shadows
Important media issues reviewed

Students are required to view and review at least three films from the following list. The reviews must deal with the portrayal of Native Americans in the film, as well as, what they feel the effects of these portrayals are on society in general.

List of Films:

Stagecoach
The Way West
Cheyenne Autumn
Soldier Blue

A Man Called Horse
Fort Apache
Little Big Man
I Will Fight No More Forever
Last of the Mohicans
Dances with Wolves

Lesson Objectives

Give students a view of the social impact of images created in the media of minorities especially Native Americans.

Students will become aware of the effects of media portrayals socially, politically, and economically.

Students will explore, in discussion and written essays, ways the media can effect change to more fairly represent Native Americans in the media.

Questions for Discussion and Possible Essay Exam

1. Is the vocabulary attributed to Native Americans in broadcast and film media demeaning? Why yes, why not? Examples?
2. Do the Indians belong to the feather-bonnet tribe? (all one big tribe syndrome)
3. What is the impact of comic interludes built upon the effects of firewater? (Interesting to note that alcohol was a problem in the U.S. Calvary)
4. Are the Indians portrayed as an extinct species?
5. Are the Indians either noble or savage?
6. Are portrayals patronizing? How so? Examples.
7. Is the Indian's humanness recognized? (Do they have homes, families, emotions other than mindless fury?)
8. Aside from the menacing chief or the lovely princess, do the Indian characters have personal names? Daily tasks? Amusements other than drinking or torturing?

Written Projects Should Include:

- An introduction with a thesis statement.
- Written reviews and evaluations of the content of each of the four chapters from *Shadows of the Indian*.
- Written two-page reviews and evaluations of the content of each of three movies from the required lists.
- Paragraphs dealing with aspects of the eight listed question above.
- Conclusion
- Works Cited Page
- Cover Page: (Title of project, student name, name of course, day and time course meets, date)
- All work should be typed, double spaced in a serif typeface.